Care, Feeding and Training of

CATS

in the Modern Manner

A HANDBOOK FOR

CAT OWNERS

by Doris Bryant

Portrait by Clare Turlay Newberry

"SNOWBALL"

Courtesy of Mrs. Elenore Amend

CONTENTS

I. A KNOWLEDGE OF CATS

THE people who have the best understanding of cats are, of course, those who have a natural love of cats.

The cat is a particularly sensitive animal, requiring much more than physical comfort for his well-being. In a quiet household, with one or two people who understand and respect cats, his charm and intelligence develop to the highest degree. Treated like people, cats actually become little people to those who love them. The real cat lover finds in his cat natural charm, graciousness, dignity and sincerity, often most regrettably lacking in human beings.

The grace of a cat as he walks, leaps, sits, or lies in repose is a great satisfaction, often filling us with awe that it should be our privilege to live in constant companionship with anything so beautiful.

For his priceless gift to us, the cat deserves the best that we can give him in sensible and intelligent care.

Two cats more satisfactory than one. Cats develop more normally with the companionship of their own kind. The devotion of two cats for each other is very deep. Get two kittens of the same or opposite sexes, have them spayed or neutered young, and there will be no question of their getting on together. It costs little more to feed two cats, and they actually are less care than one, as they are more self-sufficient. They can be left alone for longer periods without fear of their being lonely.

The exercise that two cats get in playing together is very important for their well-being. They are tremendously rough in their play, which is a natural outlet for their energy. The most important reason for having two cats is to enable them to use up this great energy on each other and not on human beings. A normal cat, taking normal exercise with another cat, should be gentle with people.

Correct treatment of cats. It is important never to be rough with cats, nor to allow them to be rough with people. Cats and human beings should treat each other with respect, always. Once this barrier is broken down, once the cat discovers he may kick and bite his human companions, he is almost sure to become rougher and rougher, until he is actually dangerous; he loses all sense of values. Once a cat has sprung at a person, he is never again an absolutely dependable pet. Many such cats have become so dangerous that it was necessary to have them put to sleep. This is deplorable, since it was not their fault that they developed as they did, but rather the fault of the people who mismanaged them. To spoil a cat's disposition is to spoil his chances of having a good home.

A cross cat is usually one that has been teased or treated roughly, or one that has been overfed. A cat must be treated with tact and consideration in order to bring out his best qualities and allow him to develop properly. A cat's dignity should never be offended. The fact that a cat does not bite or scratch or run away when he is given a rough caress or teased, does not mean he is being correctly handled; as a matter of fact, his good disposition is being ruined or he is losing confidence in people. A cat's sense of humor does not extend to having his tail pulled; anything that is an indignity will be resented by a cat. Even though some are so good-natured that they tolerate rough treatment without rebellion, it is in spite of the treatment they are receiving; these cats would have developed much more desirably had they lived with people who did not treat them thus.

Cats differ in temperament and characteristics as much as people do. It is as pitiful to see a cat living with people he does not understand and who do not understand him as it is to see people living together who are incompatible.

Nice manners from the cat's point of view. An understanding person does not attempt to pet or handle strange cats; a greeting spoken in a quiet voice, and a hand extended in friendship are all that one is permitted. The cat must decide whether the friendship is to go further.

Never pick up a cat belonging to someone else; the cat may not like it, and the owner of the cat may not like it.

People who treat their own cats with the same tactful consideration are always rewarded. Greeted by name, a cat will usually respond. Cats are affectionate and charming companions when allowed to make their own advances. Most of them like to be held or carried, once their owners have discovered just how they like to be held; some like to lie over your shoulder, some put their arms around your neck, while others just cuddle.

So much has been said and written about how to pick up a cat. It seems obvious that he should have the same comfort and sense of security while he is being picked up as when he is being held. One hand placed so he will sit on it, while the other steadies him, is a very simple method. Certainly, no cat should be picked up by the back of the neck, except in an emergency.

Cats are made nervous by noise and abrupt movements; that is why cats do not make good companions for children. It may be added, however, that cats very much enjoy any noise they themselves make!

1

APARTMENT CATS VERSUS COUNTRY CATS

People whose cats have liberty in the country feel sorry for cats confined to city apartments. Owners of apartment cats are shocked at and disapprove the risks taken by country cats.

It goes without saying that no careful person will allow a cat freedom to run on city streets.

Country cats. Country sunshine, fresh air, and an active life sometimes give a cat sufficient health and vitality to remain unharmed by the dangers constantly surrounding him.

There are few country places so far removed from all habitation that stray cats are not about. These stray cats are infested with all the parasites—fleas, ear mites, and worms; actual contact is not always necessary for transmission. Stray cats frequently have skin disorders; they may even carry the germs of such a serious cat disease as gastritis.

Dogs, cats, and rodents have the same fleas; therefore, cats can hardly go into grass without acquiring fleas.

Birds, mice, and other small animals which cats catch are not suitable food; they also give cats fleas and worms.

The cat that runs out is in danger of being run over, of getting into fights, of eating tainted or poisoned food. He may be a nuisance or a source of annoyance to neighbors.

Country cats can be kept comparatively free from parasites by a daily grooming with a flea comb and a weekly dusting with flea powder, and by periodic worming, possibly twice a year.

City cats. No other animal is so easily cared for or adapts himself so readily to city life.

Supplied with playthings, a cat will take his own exercise; two cats living together are self-sufficient. Many of the finest, healthiest cats are those living in city apartments, exposed to no dangers and no disease. They live normal, healthy, happy lives, without ever leaving their homes. Country cats can become happy apartment cats if the proper adjustment in feeding is made.

To be perfect pets, cats should be neutered. To be healthy, they should not be overfed, and their diet should not be too rich nor too stimulating.

Cats like to lie in sunny windows; cats fall out of windows and, for this reason, the windows should be fully screened.

To make up for the real country sunshine our city cats do not get, we can give them a vitamin-rich tonic now and then, during the winter and spring.

The perfect apartment pet. Cats are ideal apartment pets. There are no cleaner animals. Everyone knows that cats are fastidious, forever cleaning themselves. Even cats running out of doors are not attracted by filth, as are dogs.

A healthy, well-cared-for cat, in a clean apartment, is just about the cleanest living thing. He never so much as puts a foot on the street. He spends the greater part of his time keeping himself polished and immaculate.

2

NEUTERING AND SPAYING

Having a male cat neutered or a female cat spayed is not "cruel." It is the necessary compromise which must be made to secure a satisfactory pet and to insure the cat's own happiness under the conditions under which he is asked to live. Unaltered cats are uncertain in their habits and in their tempers; their restlessness makes them unsuitable as apartment pets.

I define a good pet as an animal that is happy and healthy, that gives pleasure and companionship with a minimum amount of trouble, and whose habits are not annoying to guests or to neighbors.

As a rule, neutered males and spayed females are healthier, and consequently are cheaper to keep. Certainly, their good manners save many cleaning bills. Unfortunately, nine out of ten neutered or spayed cats are overfed, which makes them fat and dopey—just another instance of mismanagement for which the cat pays. Properly fed neuters and spays are slim, active, playful, and keenly interested in life.

Neutering or spaying does not change the essential characteristics of a cat; it removes all of the objectionable traits and none of the desirable. It is overfeeding and wrong feeding which ruin neutered and spayed cats.

An unaltered cat is a breeding cat, whose function is to breed and who thinks of little else. The health and happiness of such a cat depend upon a normal amount of breeding. Males must have quarters, large enough for exercise, where they may spray and howl and not disturb or annoy anyone. This should not be a dark basement. A male should never be scolded or punished for doing what nature and instinct prompt him to do; he does not mean to be bad.

An unaltered male cat usually has a strong and offensive odor.

If not bred, a male may become cross and dangerous. Such a cat is not happy, and his health will suffer. Breeding him will keep him healthy, it may prevent his becoming cross, but it certainly will not keep him quiet or improve his habits; in these respects he will be worse, at least for a week or two after each breeding.

No unaltered male is absolutely reliable as to habits and temper; no matter how gentle he is he must always be watched; therefore, he is not a pet.

The crying of a female cat when she is in season is more than most people can tolerate for long. But even if the owners of the cat can stand it, she grows thin and cross from continued calling, and she too may become lax in her habits and spray on furniture or against people.

When a cat is allowed to be a nuisance, as a rule the poor cat is blamed; unthinking persons conclude that all cats are nuisances and poor pets. Those people who love cats have a great responsibility to handle them properly and keep them happy, so that they may always appear at their best before the world.

Neutering. Neutering is comparatively simple and without risk, provided the cat is taken to a good veterinarian. The best time is between three and six months of age; if the operation is properly done, the kitten does not suffer and there is no after treatment.

Some people do not have male cats neutered until they are a year old, in order that they may acquire the massive head and shoulders which male kittens neutered young do not get. A male cat may be neutered when several years old. However, a male of a year or more may have acquired some traits which neutering will not change.

Spaying. The spaying of females is a major surgical operation, by which the ovaries are removed. Some risk is involved even when the operation is done by an expert under favorable conditions. All too often a cat is allowed to become worn out and depleted by constant calling or by too much kitten bearing; it is unkind to the cat and unfair to the veterinarian who is to spay her to let this happen. People should know what they are doing when they acquire a female cat or kitten; even when a female cat is accidentally acquired, the responsibility is no less—the cat must be bred, or spayed, or properly put to sleep—but *never* just passed on to someone else.

A female kitten may be spayed at any age after four months, depending upon when the veterinarian wishes to take her. It seldom is, but may be done quite late in a cat's life; spaying at four or five years of age is common. It may be done after a cat has had any number of kittens; however, her milk must be entirely dried up when she goes to be spayed. She cannot be spayed when in season without extreme risk. Cats that have a cystic condition of the ovaries come into season and stay in; in such cases there is nothing to do but take the risk and have them spayed.

The female is given a general anesthetic and does not suffer. She remains in the hospital for at least five days; the wound where the incision is made must be dressed daily until it heals and the stitches can be removed. She returns home thin and must be treated as a convalescent. Be sure to find out if she has yet taken solid food, and be guided by the section on Convalescent Feeding.

A spayed female requires much less food than one that is not spayed. Females have trimmer and more youthful lines after they are spayed, if they are not overfed. They are charming, playful, lithe animals—unequaled pets.

The peculiar cry used when a cat is in season is made at no other time; it will not be heard after a cat is spayed. Being nervous and upset, the cat may cry rather badly for a week or two after she returns from being spayed; if it lasts longer than that she is lonely, or just a noisy cat.

Some female cats are never troublesome and do not have to be spayed. This is exceptional, and is not true of the general run of female cats.

3

CAT PSYCHOLOGY

A cat lives in a make-believe world of adventure. Whether this is due to his natural wisdom or to his perfect adjustment to domestic life, at any rate it enables him to keep completely happy and healthy. He stretches and he runs and he keeps his fine body in good condition. He scratches and sharpens his claws as diligently as if he might need them at any moment to engage in desperate combat. He pretends his playthings are alive, and the game is tireless and all-absorbing. His life is filled to the brim with fun and activity and intense living. Whether he is playing or investigating or just meditating, he lives fully and completely and happily in the moment. If you are handling your cat properly, he will not lose these qualities as he grows older.

Many cats have a very lively and subtle sense of humor.

Change. The most difficult thing for a cat is making any sort of change. He likes to do the same things day after day, and if you observe your cat closely you will discover how much he functions on a schedule. We try never to make too many changes at one time, and not to introduce too many strange things into a cat's life without time in between for adjustment. If a cat must go to a new home, it is enough that he become acquainted with one room and one person first; gradually his horizon may be widened. Even when a cat is moving with his own family, it is kind and wise to confine him first to one room and give him more freedom as he feels safe and at home.

The matter of making all change gradual applies to everything that happens to cats. They should not be subjected to extremes in temperature or radical changes in diet. A change may precipitate some trouble already imminent.

The cat's attitude. The cat is an intelligent animal and he likes to please—provided he also pleases himself. In other words, he is no more selfish than human beings, but he never stoops to hypocrisy. He refuses to flatter and he is never servile.

A cat is capable of deep devotion to a person, but his devotion depends upon his approval; his utter lack of flattery makes his devotion something worth cherishing.

4

DISCIPLINE

A cat cannot be forced to do anything, but he can be coaxed and he can be trained. Tact, restraint, and gentleness are always necessary when dealing with cats. They respond most of all to one's voice.

A cat can be trained to have nice manners and not to damage or injure things in a house, provided he is allowed an outlet for his natural instincts. A cat must run, leap, scratch his claws, and sit on high places. His health and happiness, as well as his good manners, depend upon a normal outlet in these matters.

When two cats live together, running and play are

taken care of without any supervision from human beings. A cat living alone should be provided with interesting toys, and some time must be devoted to him each day; a bedtime romp is customary in most households.

If a cat is permitted certain chairs or tables or a mantle on which he may perch without being scolded, he can be trained to stay off certain other places.

The claw scratching is, of course, a matter of supplying him with something to use, as a cat must sharpen his claws. Scolding him for using the furniture, when nothing has been provided for his use, is thoughtless and cruel, or at least shows ignorance regarding cats.

For the most part, discipline is maintained by the cat over his human companions. A cat does the same thing at the same time every day and he likes people to arrange their lives in like manner; many cats refuse to permit late sleeping on Sundays and holidays.

Cats are capable of weekly as well as daily schedules. A cat that was receiving a weekly treatment for ear mites knew when the day came round and hid immediately after breakfast; he did not like the treatments. Another cat customarily spent Sunday morning helping the man of the house read the Sunday paper; he approved of those quiet, lazy hours. One day the man stayed home from the office in the middle of the week and, although he sat in the same chair, and read the newspaper, the cat would not go near him; he was displeased and he refused to be friendly. His schedule had been upset!

5

TRAINING

Cats can be trained by those who understand cat psychology. It is largely a matter of making it possible for them to do the right things, and impossible for them to do the things you do not wish done. Experienced persons know what mistakes to look for and try to prevent their happening. If a mistake is made, it should not be allowed to be repeated, and all possibility of its repetition must be eliminated for a long period of time. *The longer a bad habit has been indulged, the longer it requires to correct it.* That means a longer period when the cat has no opportunity to repeat the mistake. Bad habits, such as not using a pan properly, cannot be allowed to extend over many weeks; if they are, correction may not be possible.

Scolding a cat after he has done something wrong does no good, and injures his disposition; he does not connect the punishment with the thing done; therefore, he is either resentful or frightened or has his feelings hurt. There are no conditions or circumstances under which a cat may be struck or severely punished; it serves no good purpose and hurts his disposition; it frightens him and destroys his trust in people, thus making any future training more difficult, if not impossible.

It is entirely permissible and most effective to scold a cat and give him a little smack *when he is about to do something wrong*; in such cases he does get the connection. If he is a timid and sensitive cat, whose feelings are easily hurt, he can immediately be picked up and petted or given something gay and interesting to do.

It is convenient, particularly when kittens are growing up, to keep an interesting toy laid aside, but quickly available, to distract a cat's attention at critical moments.

While successful training must begin in kittenhood, grown cats always need some supervision to prevent their acquiring bad habits. If such a habit starts, either the cat must be removed from the temptation, or the temptation removed from the cat, until such time as he has forgotten about it and the instinct has been satisfied in some other way, or diverted to the proper procedure. Prompt action is necessary before the habit becomes firmly set. All cats must be watched when a new article of furniture is brought into the house, as their natural instinct is to try it out for claw scratching. Supervise their inspection, and do not leave them alone in the room with it until after they have ceased to regard it as something new.

A cat happily occupied in a natural way will easily be guided from the things it is not convenient to have him do. Such annoying habits as tearing paper and climbing up people or curtains are acquired in kittenhood; they should not be tolerated.

The first six months of a kitten's life is the formative or training period. Properly handled during this time, a kitten has every chance of developing into a well-mannered cat, charming to live with, and to be trusted to do no damage in any home surroundings.

Since a kitten usually goes to his new home under six months of age, his training is only begun by the breeder; it must be continued by the new owner.

Both cats and kittens learn the meaning of "don't," "stop it," or some such phrase. This method of control works well with grown cats, as well as telling them in a hurt voice how bad they are. Kittens, however, are so active that they can do ten wrong things in five minutes; during particularly active moments a cage or playroom is imperative.

A cage is often a great convenience, particularly for those owning more than one cat. Cats should be accustomed to cages so that they can be put into them when they become ill or when they must be boarded. If not accustomed to a cage a cat will fuss and be very unhappy. The easiest way to get a cat to like a cage is to feed him in it; or just leave the door open—you will find him sleeping in it.

Nice manners make a cat a perfect pet; bad manners make him a pest. If a cat is spoiled, someone must have spoiled him. A cat with nice manners gets better treatment from the world, and since his manners depend upon the person who trained him, that person is largely responsible for his well-being during his whole life. Undoing the mistakes of a previous owner requires all the tact, patience, and perseverance of a person who *really* understands and loves cats.

It need hardly be said that one should be consistent in handling a cat; do not permit him to do a thing one day and scold him for it the next. Moreover, all members of a household must be perfectly agreed on just what a cat may do and how he is to be corrected.

Things a cat cannot be trained to do. There are certain compromises which cat owners must make; one must learn to be watchful regarding certain things. Cats simply will get under foot, dash through doors, and fall out of windows. They are curious, and an open closet door or bureau drawer is an invitation they cannot resist. Cats or kittens will leap out of your arms unexpectedly; small kittens may be injured by so great a fall; if the leap was caused by sudden panic, you may be badly scratched by the back claws, particularly if they are not clipped. The cat is a nervous animal, quickly and easily frightened; sometimes he seems to become frightened at nothing at all, and he may remain in a state of panic for several hours or even days. People owning several cats may have the whole lot of them go into panic, making it necessary to confine them separately until they have recovered their normal senses. The yowling and hair-raising at such a time are unequaled on any alley fence. Cats in such a state should not be fed.

Needles and pins must never be dropped or left about; cats play with them and usually swallow them.

Cats can never be trusted in the matter of food. A cat can be trained to stay off tables when there is someone in the room, but he cannot be trusted to do so when there is no person present. Siamese have a strong preference for kitchens and must be watched particularly in the matter of appropriating food.

While it is well known that cats can be careful, it is also well known that they may not always be so. Sometimes they leap for a table, miss, and drag everything on it with them to the floor. A valuable vase may stand safely on the mantel for five years, and then one day be knocked down by the cat.

Sanitary pan. Cats take to a sanitary pan quite readily; kittens frequently learn to use a pan of their own accord. A mistake is sometimes made when a cat or kitten goes into a new home; this is due to nervousness and confusion; the new owner should prevent such an accident by not giving the new pet too much freedom at first. If a mistake is made it is usually on a bed, divan or rug, or in the bath tub. A cat can be shut away from the first three; water can be left in the tub.

Things used in sanitary pans are sand, sawdust, peat moss, and newspaper. By far the most common is newspaper. Several thicknesses are spread on the bottom of the pan and strips of paper torn to fill the pan. This gives the cat something in which to scratch.

A pan should be changed as often as it is used, and thoroughly cleansed with hot water. If this is done, disinfectants and deodorants will not be necessary, except in cases of sickness or with unaltered male cats; in such cases the proper disinfectant should be employed each time the pan is used, and should also be used in wiping up around the pan. Pans not properly cared for acquire an offensive odor and attract roaches and other household insects. Cats are fastidious, and many have acquired bad habits because they have refused to use pans not changed often enough.

Do not try to make your cat use too small a pan. Large apartments and houses should have more than one. A cat must never be shut away from his pan.

When a cat has used a rug instead of his pan, it is necessary to have the rug cleaned, so that no odor remains to attract the cat. It is advisable to leave the rug up for several weeks or months, so the cat will have forgotten about using it. In the case of beds or chairs, everything must go to the cleaners and the cat must be kept from that room until he is using his pan properly elsewhere. If a cat really wants to use one corner of the room, a pan can be placed there.

If lax habits are not quickly checked, putting the cat into a cage when he cannot be watched is the only possible method of handling the situation. Half-way methods will never suffice.

One important reason for not selling a kitten under three months is that his habits regarding the use of his pan are not well established under that age.

Do not mistake the spraying of males, and of females when in season, for bad manners. This is something quite natural to them and cannot be controlled.

Claw sharpening. This is a natural instinct which cannot be curbed or checked. The wise and normal thing is to encourage it and praise the cat each time you

Photograph by Tod and Mina

SEAL POINT SIAMESE

Courtesy of Mrs. Milton Erlanger

see him using the log or scratching board provided for that purpose. A kitten that grows up with only logs to use, with careful introduction into rooms where there is upholstered furniture, is the cat most likely to have good manners. Cats that have used furniture and rugs can seldom be enticed back to wood; carpet-covered scratching boards and posts have been invented for their use, nicely filled with catnip, and inviting to any cat. If praised for using one of these, and scolded for using the furniture, any cat can soon be induced to use one exclusively, particularly if he is put to sleep where there is nothing else to use for claw sharpening—for all cats sharpen their claws upon awakening.

Many people provide a log or scratching board in every room; certainly large apartments and houses should have more than one. Be sure to obtain those heavy enough so the cat cannot pull them over; a cat seldom goes back to a scratching post he has pulled over.

Chewing cloth. Chewing and eating blankets and towels is about the most annoying habit a cat can have, and it certainly is not good for him. No matter what the cause, it becomes a habit unless quickly checked.

Kittens going too young into new homes frequently start chewing and eating their bedding; kittens backward about eating often start it. Some deficiency in diet, particularly calcium deficiency, is a cause. Boredom is a common cause. The habit may start during the teething period.

All kittens will eat wool; for this reason woolen blankets should never be used in their beds.

If some careless person has sold you a kitten with this chewing habit, you will have untold expense and trouble. You may at any time find a hole in your expensive blankets or your best dress.

Keeping cats amused. Good health means an abundance of energy. Healthy cats are never too old to play.

Playthings should be rotated. It is a good idea to keep a drawer for them, leaving it open just enough so the cats must work to get the things out. This is a game of which they never tire.

Some cats and all kittens are fascinated by the spot of light reflected by the sun on a mirror. Kittens get endless fun from a hand mirror left on the floor.

Tricks. There are certain tricks which come quite naturally to cats; we can encourage the ones for which our cats show an aptitude.

Opening doors is not a trick we wish to encourage, but many cats seem to do very well without any help and in spite of discouragement.

The urge to climb a person's clothing seems quite different from the willingness to leap into one's arms. This urge to climb clothing can and should be discouraged; clipping the claws of kittens is the first step. Those cats that show a desire to jump into one's arms always give warning of their intention; the habit can be fostered by standing before a door the cat wishes to go through, and coaxing him to jump. Many kittens learn quite easily to jump up into one's hands.

Retrieving comes naturally to kittens and many learn with no help. Supplying them with playthings which they can carry in their mouths is the first step. If you notice your kitten taking a certain plaything to a certain part of the room, go there and sit near and, each time he arrives, pet him, pretend he brought the plaything to you, and throw it for him. He will get the idea quickly.

Siamese kittens enjoy retrieving; blankets, towels,

scrub cloths and dish mops must be kept beyond their reach. There is no more comical sight than a cross-eyed Siamese kitten, with terribly intent and serious expression, stumbling over a full-sized bed blanket which he is trying to take somewhere.

II. GENERAL CARE

CORRECT feeding is the most important thing in the care of cats. The next in importance is effective grooming.

It cannot be stressed too strongly that needles, pins, thread, string, elastic and elastic bands should not be left where cats can get them. Like babies, they will put anything into their mouths; it is a real tragedy when some of the above-mentioned articles have been swallowed.

1

FEEDING

Wrong feeding and overfeeding are the causes of most of the ills which befall cats.

Special feeding of breeding cats, very young kittens, and of invalids is discussed elsewhere in this book.

The feeding of pet cats—neutered males and spayed females—is simple. They do not require much variety. The object is to keep them trim and graceful with a diet not too stimulating for apartment cats; this promotes good health. A fat cat is not beautiful, is apt to be cross, and has little resistance against disease. An overfed cat is inactive.

The amount given at a feeding must be decided by the owner of each cat. A cat should be neither fat nor pathetically thin. A tiny, nervous, active cat sometimes eats more than a large and placid cat. The average normal cat receives two meals daily; he is usually fed the first thing in the morning and at the dinner hour in the evening.

A cat must be kept interested in his food *not* by seeking new things to tempt him, but by feeding sensible food in amounts small enough to insure his being always ready for the next meal. A normal, healthy cat takes a normal and healthy interest in wholesome and sensible food. A cat should not be screaming while his food is being prepared; this means he is too hungry or his diet is wrong and not supplying his needs; or it means he is a noisy and unpleasant cat.

Many foods popularly given cats have little nourishment, and many lack elements necessary for a cat's well-being.

A normal kitten of three months is given three meals daily and all the milk he wants, provided that much milk is not too laxative. He is permitted longer to eat his meals because he may rush off to play before he has really finished. The first thing in the morning, late afternoon, and bedtime are suitable and convenient feeding hours for kittens. If a kitten has a good romp in the evening and a meal just before he is put to bed, he will probably sleep all night and disturb no one.

A kitten cuts his second teeth between four and seven months of age; some are upset by teething and some are not. Usually they require soft food, but if a kitten seems to crave something hard to chew, some large lumps of Kibbled food will not hurt him. If a kitten refuses to eat, have a look at his teeth before assuming he is ill; possibly there is a tooth hanging loose which you can help him get out.

The age at which a cat changes from three to two meals a day must be at the discretion of the owner. Usually it is some time between six and twelve months of age, although some frail cats with dainty appetites have three meals all their lives. A very active, growing kitten eats a large amount of food and remains quite thin; his requirements are really greater than those of a grown spayed or neutered cat. A cat can be cut to two meals when he becomes fat or inactive, or rather, just before that happens.

Regularity in hours of feeding is advisable, but not absolutely essential in the case of grown, healthy cats. The owner of a well-cared-for cat need not rush home just to give the cat his dinner. The cat may just as well be fed at a later hour, provided suitable food is available then. A *too* well-cared-for cat may miss a meal entirely now and then with beneficial results.

The idea that cats know what is good for them is a fallacy. Cats have been known to eat olives, nuts, doughnuts, elastic bands, cigarettes, cigarette ashes, coffee, and chewing gum. It is quite likely that a craving for abnormal things indicates a deficiency in the cat's diet and a veterinarian should be consulted regarding a corrective diet.

Foods which have no particular food value and which cats like too well, such as shrimps, tinned salmon, and liver, may well be avoided. Cats hold out for them and get so they will eat nothing else. The fact that some cats are fed exclusively on any one of the foods just mentioned does not indicate the food is suitable or that the cats are perfectly well or will remain so. Having nothing else to do, they can to some extent sleep off the ill effects of wrong feeding. But of what use either to themselves or their owners are cats that sleep all the time?

Sometimes nervousness and a twitching skin are the first manifestations of improper feeding. Rough, uneven coat, bare patches, ears completely bare of fur, and eczema result from the exclusive feeding of tinned food, from too much starchy food, and from overfeeding of too rich foods.

Almost invariably a wrongly fed cat has a strong and offensive odor about his body and his sanitary pan. This is also true of a sick cat. A healthy, properly fed altered cat has no odor about his body or his pan.

A properly fed cat is eager for each meal and eats with relish. His coat is glossy, his body slim and active, his breath sweet.

Proper and sensible feeding is economical; it cuts down the cost of food and avoids veterinary bills.

What to feed. Beef is generally considered the best and most essential food for cats and should form the foundation of all diets. Milk is a natural food for cats. Beef is constipating; milk is laxative; it is possible to feed a cat on just these two things, and keep him regular. Over a long period of time cats have been found to become bored with just beef and milk, unless kept extremely thin and hungry.

As a supplementary food to use with beef, a good dry prepared cat food is economical, gives excellent results, keeps a cat regular and holds a cat's interest in his food. Such a food cuts down the richness and stimulating effect of beef and provides a balanced diet.

Vegetables are not an important nor a natural food for cats. However, many cats like them, and seem better satisfied with their food when some vegetable is mixed with their beef once or twice a week. The prepared cat food should be omitted from the meals when vegetables are given. Vegetables suitable for cats are the non-starchy varieties such as spinach, string beans, asparagus, celery, lettuce—those that grow above the ground. These should all be fresh and they should be cooked.

Vegetables are usually laxative. They have not been found satisfactory for kittens under five or six months of age.

Most cats like broth. It should be made at home; particularly for invalids and kittens, all fat should be removed. Prepared cat food made in broth instead of water is a nice in-between meal for kittens.

Fish is an excellent food for healthy cats. Sick cats, convalescents, and kittens under five months should not have fish. Heavy, oily varieties should be avoided. Fresh codfish is most desirable; boil, and do not over-cook; to make sure there are no bones, it should be gone through twice. Fish so frequently disagrees with cats when mixed with other foods that a safe rule is to feed it always alone.

Eggs are suitable food for cats; raw or lightly cooked, they may be used instead of beef. They are definitely a building-up food; the average cat should not have them too often, preferably in winter.

Lean, cooked meat or fowl left over from the family table may be minced, and mixed with the prepared cat food to make a meal for a cat. If these are fed without the cat food, the cat may like them too well and hold out for them; besides, they are more suitable when mixed with the cat food. A wholesome diet promotes a wholesome appetite.

Titbits and treats should be given only after the regular meal, and not too frequently. Many cats like cheese.

Catnip. Catnip is a tonic herb, attractive to most cats; they may have all they want.

If cats tear and chew their catnip toys, it is usually an indication they are starved for catnip.

If kittens pay no attention to catnip it is because they are young; they probably will like it as they grow older.

Cats deprived of catnip for a long period will overindulge when first it is given them; they will get excited or even intoxicated. Cats accustomed to a little every day seldom get excited and seldom eat much at one time. They really enjoy rolling in it as much as eating it.

In handling breeding stock it should be remembered that catnip is an aphrodisiac.

Feeding rules. Keep fresh water where a cat can get to it at all times. Change once or twice daily, thoroughly cleansing the bowl each time.

Feeding dishes must be clean and sanitary. If the same size dish is always used it is quite easy to estimate the amount of food without weighing.

Food must be room temperature or warmer; *icy cold food should never be given.*

Two or more cats may sometimes eat from one dish; usually it is advisable to feed in separate dishes, and some cats do better when fed in separate cages or rooms.

Thirty minutes is quite long enough to leave food down; what is uneaten should be thrown out. Unless the cat is sick or overfed, or protesting at the introduction of some new food, there will be no food left, and it will be eaten in five minutes. If a cat refuses his regular food, there must be a reason. Don't give anything else. Just omit the meal, watch him closely, and try to determine the cause. It may be that he is overfed, or he may not be feeling well; in either case, no food at all is advisable. The next meal must be given only if he is anxious for it, and it must be smaller than usual, or he may not retain it.

If a cat eats too fast, spread his food over a large plate.

Wipe up every trace of food a cat may have spilled on the floor around his dish. These food particles attract insects, and they will do the cat no good if he eats them hours later when the food has spoiled.

Food must be absolutely fresh. With the cat's sensitive stomach and tendency to gastritis, nothing is so important as fresh food. Special attention must be paid to the purchasing of the cat's beef. Hamburger is dangerous because it may have tainted meat in it, because it is usually too fat, and because ground raw beef should be fed immediately after grinding. Even selecting the meat and having the butcher grind it is dangerous, as what first comes from the grinder may have been standing there several hours.

Unless you are fortunate enough to live near a market that carries bull meat for dogs and cats, top round is about the most economical cut, as there is little waste. Wash the meat before grinding and cut away gristle, discolored parts, and most of the fat. Whether or not any fat is included would depend upon the time of year and the condition of the cat.

Ground beef is best for cats; if it is fed in chunks or pieces, cats do not and cannot chew it properly; sometimes they vomit the chunks; frequently improperly chewed beef causes diarrhea. Ground beef is more easily digested and better assimilated; grinding beef makes it possible to mix it thoroughly with other foods. It would be far better to give beef in one large chunk than cut in pieces, for then the cat would have to chew, thus stimulating the flow of saliva and furnishing the teeth some beneficial exercise.

If the beef purchased is very fresh and in one large piece, several meals of raw meat can be served, cutting off just enough for each meal, grinding, and feeding immediately. Daily inspection of beef soon makes one expert regarding its freshness and at estimating just how many meals of raw meat can be fed before the remainder of the beef is boiled, ground, and set aside on the ice. The feeding of cooked beef is so quick and easy that it is compensation for the extra trouble taken in preparing the raw beef meals. Cooked beef seems just as good for cats as raw beef; in the case of invalids, it is better. Cooked meat keeps well and it doesn't require much planning to have it available for the cats on Sundays and holidays.

Vegetables must be put through the grinder or finely minced; otherwise, they will be neither properly chewed nor properly digested.

If dry prepared cat food is fed in conjunction with beef, it is prepared by pouring the correct amount for the feeding into a pan of boiling water, and letting it boil until the water is absorbed. The food should be fluffy and palatable. It is important to select a good quality food which contains no splintered bones and which is not heavy and thick when prepared in water.

As the meat is always cold and the cat food hot from the stove, mixing them together gives a meal of about the right temperature. The proportion of prepared food to beef varies with the individual cat; the prepared food should not form more than half the diet, rather less. It gives bulk and is fed in sufficient quantity to insure a daily, well-formed bowel movement.

Suggested feeding schedule for altered cats. Feed two meals daily. For each meal boil a heaping teaspoonful of prepared cat food in water, and mix with about one and one-half ounces of beef. Add two or three pieces of Kibbled food for the teeth. If a cat is not overfed, he will accept a dish of milk daily. Put milk down regularly, night and morning, until you discover at which time the cat prefers it. A little cream may be added to the milk. For variety, fresh codfish may be given once a week, and vegetables may be substituted for cat food once or twice a week. (Some people feed beef one meal and cat food the other—instead of mixing them.) In extremely hot weather feed even more lightly, but give no cold food.

What not to feed. Never feed starchy food, such as potatoes, rice, corn, beets, pastry, and white bread; never feed raw vegetables; avoid strong seasoning. Don't economize by buying beef head or lungs; these will give your cats worms.

Strong white teeth. Since cats' teeth have no daily brushing and since most of their food is soft, how are teeth to be kept strong, white, and in good condition? It is very difficult to be entirely successful in this matter, but there are certain things which help. To begin with, if a cat was fed calcium through the seventh month, and his mother was also fed calcium, he started life with sound teeth. To keep these teeth in condition some hard food is necessary. Every firm manufacturing a dry prepared cat food also manufactures a Kibbled food, which is in quite large pieces and very hard. This is safe for cats; bones are not. Never give a cat bones from the table.

Making a change in diet. Do not conclude because a cat refuses something once that that is final. At a different time he may like it very much. Also do not conclude that a certain food does not agree with a cat if he vomits it the first time it is given to him; he may simply have eaten it too fast, or he may not have been feeling well that day.

It is quite possible to make a change in the diet of a cat no matter how spoiled he is or how set he may be in his ways. Attempting to starve a cat into eating something is useless, as he loses all urge to eat after he has fasted for several days. The starving must be gradual.

To the food a cat likes and is accustomed to, add very small amounts of the desired food; gradually increase the amount of one, while decreasing the amount of the other. Keep him hungry with smaller and smaller meals; a keen edge to his appetite will induce him to accept what is given him.

This procedure may safely be followed with normal, healthy cats; overfed cats should profit by it. Delicate cats, with dainty appetites, usually require a tonic to improve their general condition and stimulate their appetites before they can be disciplined in the matter of food.

Even if a cat will accept an abrupt change in diet, it is wiser to make the change gradual.

No great change is advocated in the diet of a pet cat of eight or ten years of age, provided he has done well on the diet to which he has been accustomed. If, however, such a cat has been overfed, it should be possible to add many years to his life by a change to light feeding.

Fussy eaters. There are a few delicate cats with dainty appetites that actually have to be coaxed and pampered. In the majority of cases a fussy eater is just a spoiled and overfed cat.

2

GROOMING

Brushing invigorates the skin and coat; a short-haired cat should be sleek and glossy; a long-haired cat should be fluffy. A good coat comes from good health and proper grooming. Cats are in poor coat and have poor coloring during the summer months.

The main reason for brushing and combing cats is to remove as much loose hair as possible; even the most carefully groomed cats swallow some hair when washing themselves.

Effective elimination of loose hair requires a special comb or brush, suited to the length and thickness of your cat's fur. Animal combs are made of metal and have set-in teeth; ordinary combs cannot compare with them for effectiveness.

A cat should be groomed every day. A perfectly groomed cat does not leave much hair about the house.

Long-haired cats are combed the right way, to eliminate loose hair, and are brushed the wrong way, to make them fluffy. If you have acquired a neglected Long-Hair you may have to cut out the mats.

If you have acquired a grown cat that objects to grooming, your problem is very great and very tragic, as far as the cat is concerned. Holding a cat by force to groom him is the wrong method of handling; it usually just makes him worse. With infinite patience, grooming him only when he is sleepy and relaxed, and never working too long at one time, every effort should be made to convince the cat that grooming is really a pleasant experience.

Grooming kittens. Kittens shed very little but they roll about and get quite dirty; they can be wiped with a damp cloth and brushed until dry. This will teach them from earliest kittenhood what it means to be groomed; they will learn to accept it and enjoy it. To keep kittens presentable it is usually necessary to clean them daily and to wipe the dust and wax from their ears. Do not hold and groom them when they are anxious to play.

Bathing. It is not natural for a cat to be bathed and, since he seldom gets dirty next to the skin, there is no reason for soaking him. Too much bathing dries out the skin and coat. With the exception of all-white cats living in cities, no cat should need regular bathing. The surface dirt can be wiped off with a damp cloth and the cat brushed until dry; the slight dampness aids in removing loose hair. Rubbing alcohol may be added to the water if a disinfectant is required.

If a cat is bathed, a pure white baby soap should be used; the cat should not be permitted to get chilled or catch cold.

A cat is as clean as the floor he plays on.

3

CLAWS

The cat's sharp claws were intended for defense against his enemies and for climbing away from them to safety. Cats having their liberty in town or country still need their claws for these purposes.

In the case of house cats never allowed out of doors, the matter is quite different. They have nothing from which to defend themselves and any tendency to climb drapes and curtains can hardly be tolerated if a cat is to be a satisfactory pet.

The claws of a house cat grow abnormally long; cats living out of doors wear their claws off on stones and other hard surfaces. The very long and excessively sharp claws of house cats not only catch in drapes, pillows and clothing, but sometimes grow back into the foot, causing painful sores. A cat handles himself better with clipped claws, and it takes not more than a day for him to get used to having them clipped.

The saving to clothing and the comfort of not being accidentally scratched are reasons enough for cutting the claws of house cats.

There is no connection between the sharpening of claws and the cutting of claws. The instinct to sharpen claws is just as keen whether they are sharp or blunt; the up-keep of scratching boards and posts will be considerably less when claws are clipped!

Ordinary scissors shatter the claws. For the price of having your cat's claws clipped once you can buy a neat little pair of clippers, made for cats, easy and safe to use.

Cats' claws shed by scaling off on each side. The cats break these layers loose when sharpening their claws; they also pull them off with their teeth.

Uncut claws are dangerous for cats that climb screen doors; many of them have gotten claws caught and twisted their legs badly.

Photograph by Tod and Mina

LONG-HAIRED CATS

Courtesy of Miss Mary Porter and Miss Mary Dewson

III. FIRST AID IN EMERGENCIES

In most emergencies the cat should be placed immediately in his cage, where he will be quiet and can be closely watched.

Bites and scratches of another animal. Apply Dr. Camuti's antiseptic oil, and do not permit the cat to wash it right off. Watch the wounds, and if infection starts have your veterinarian advise you. If the bite is inflicted by a stray dog or cat there is the possibility of rabies, and you should see your veterinarian at once.

Injured eye, such as scratch of another cat, or something dropped into the eye. Borofax or Butyn Ointment will soothe the eye until the veterinarian can care for it. When several cats are living together, it is safest to keep the claws clipped.

Overeating of stolen food, such as a roast. Give milk of magnesia and do not feed for a day.

Overeating of stolen food, such as fowl. If bones have been eaten, a lubricant (mineral oil, vaseline, or Laxamel) is advisable. Do not feed for a day.

Bone or needle in the throat. Keep the cat quiet until the veterinarian arrives.

When thread, twine, cloth, steel wool, broom straws, or any such thing has been eaten. Give lubricant. If the foreign matter is not passed, your veterinarian should be advised of the fact.

Poison. Only a veterinarian can do anything for the cat.

Vomiting. See section on Gastritis.

Fit or convulsion. Keep as quiet as possible, or leave alone, until the veterinarian arrives.

Panic. Keep quiet or leave alone. If in two or three hours the cat appears to get worse instead of better, have the veterinarian in. A cat may salivate from fear.

Lameness, or broken bone from fall. Keep confined and quiet until the veterinarian arrives.

Paralysis. Is present in some infectious diseases. Most common causes are chronic constipation, autointoxication, and poisoning. In kittens, it may be rickets; in nursing mother cats, it may be eclampsia.

Chill. Keep warm and quiet. Withhold food, or give warm fluid.

Burn. Apply Carron Oil or any common household oil, and try to keep on a light bandage. If the burn is serious or extensive, the veterinarian should see the cat as soon as possible. Cats have been seriously burned by jumping on hot stoves and on hot gas ovens.

Emergency remedies. The above suggestions indicate the most important emergency remedies to have on hand.

IV. "DON'TS"

Don't assume that because your cat has always been well he cannot get sick.

Don't assume that any theory or any method of feeding or care is right for all cats because it happens to have been successful for one or two or a dozen. Accurate information regarding cats is not arrived at in such manner.

Don't let druggists and friends prescribe for your cat; only a competent veterinarian is qualified.

Don't give your cat castor oil or other laxatives intended for human beings.

Never give dog medicines to cats, nor use flea powders or soaps intended for dogs.

Don't use kerosene, turpentine, gasoline, or any cleaning fluid on a cat; if he gets something on him which can't be washed off it must be cut off, sacrificing his fur and good looks for a time.

Don't use any household insecticide or disinfectant unless you know it is harmless to cats. Insecticides poisonous to cats should not be used in buildings where cats live, as roaches go from one apartment to another. Eating a roach that has run through such powder can give a cat gastritis.

A cat should not eat flies or other insects.

Never use coal tar or carbolic acid products on or near a cat.

Don't leave razor blades or sharp knives about.

Don't permit a cat to eat flowers, plants, or green cut boughs from the country; some of these things are toxic; they may be covered with a poisonous spray. Cats sometimes chew and eat the wood of branches; these sharp splinters are most dangerous. Don't leave pins, needles or thread about.

If your cat is clean and healthy, do not bring in another cat with parasites or one that is not in every way as clean and healthy as your own.

If a mother cat is deprived suddenly of all her kittens, provision must be made for drying up her milk.

Don't acquire a female cat or kitten unless you are willing to take the responsibility of having her spayed, or of breeding her regularly and properly.

Don't feed a cat that is nervous. Never feed a cat within four or five hours before or after a journey. Feeding when nervous will only cause indigestion, which may possibly lead to gastritis.

Don't let a sick cat eat grass.

Don't give olive oil to your cat; it is not a medicine; and it is neither an ideal food nor an ideal lubricant.

Don't assume that your cat has worms because he is not well; above all, do not worm a sick cat.

Don't upset a sick cat further by taking him to the doctor; have the doctor in.

Don't overfeed.

Don't try to economize with cheap food, cheap doctors, and cheap boarding kennels. There is no surer way of getting into expensive trouble.

Don't say you do not believe in veterinarians because you happen to have encountered some who did not understand cats, or because you let your cat get too sick before calling the veterinarian. Find a good cat veterinarian before your cat gets sick; call him at once when anything seems wrong.

Cats suggest the mysterious, but do not let this lead

you to a belief that their care and handling are a mystery. An understanding of cats and a knowledge of cats are matters of experience, possible only to those who love cats and who live and work in constant association with them.

V. DISEASES OF THE CAT

It is common knowledge that cats are sensitive animals, difficult to treat when they become ill. Fear and unhappiness often prevent the recovery of a cat. Veterinarians who understand cats recommend that they be treated in their own homes, knowing the chances of recovery are much greater.

If you own a cage, and your cat is accustomed to staying in it, he can be placed there the instant you discover he is not well. In no other way can a sick cat be properly handled.

The most common serious diseases of the cat are gastritis, gastro-enteritis, head and chest infections, and their complications. Every cat owner should know the essential precautions to take to prevent these diseases, what the symptoms are, and what action to take when such symptoms appear. The actual treatment of these diseases must be in the hands of a good veterinarian, and he positively must be called at once.

It is of paramount importance to keep cats away from places where germs of serious diseases may be.

As for the diseases a cat seldom gets—it seems rather futile and altogether confusing for a cat owner to do much delving into the details of these; if a cat comes down with one, a veterinarian must be called anyway.

Treatment. When a cat becomes ill, no matter what is the matter with him, a dose of milk of magnesia is always the first step.

Call the veterinarian at once. Don't expect a veterinarian to be a magician. The cat is a most difficult animal to treat; and animals can't talk and tell you how they feel. It follows, therefore, that a veterinarian treating a cat is entitled to every consideration and the sympathetic understanding and cooperation of the owner of the cat. The owner must be a good nurse, keep accurate records, and report to the doctor often by telephone. In serious illnesses it is necessary for the doctor to see the cat once or twice daily for the first few days.

Several of Dr. Louis J. Camuti's remedies for cats are recommended in this book because they have proved outstandingly successful, and because *they are absolutely safe for cats.*

1

GASTRITIS AND GASTRO-ENTERITIS

Generally speaking, there is no such thing as a cat being "off his feed," unless, of course, he is hopelessly overfed, and that in itself is dangerous. If a cat does not eat his regular food, it is usually a serious symptom, particularly if he sits about and is less active than usual. All food and water should be removed and milk of magnesia given; if he seems definitely "dumpy" get the veterinarian at once. If he vomits, start giving Dr. Camuti's Prescription No. 1, or whatever nausea tablet you use, until your veterinarian can take the case.

Causes. There are infectious and non-infectious types of gastritis and gastro-enteritis. As a cat may die within twenty-four hours from the time you first notice he is not well, it is worth while to make every effort not to expose your cat to the infectious types of these diseases. The non-infectious types are caused by wrong feeding, overfeeding, tainted food, splintered bones, icy cold food, nervousness, chill, etc. Very often an illness is brought on by a combination of two or more of the things mentioned above. For instance, feeding a nervous cat, or one that has been chilled or badly frightened, may cause a slight gastric upset; continuing to feed such a cat may result in gastritis. Toxic, overfed cats succumb to gastritis easily, and have little resistance against it.

Symptoms. Loss of appetite, excessive drinking of water, refusal to play or to purr, spiky fur, and lying on the stomach with feet tucked under in front are all symptoms of a gastric upset. There is usually vomiting; sometimes the cat loses a meal hours after it was eaten, and continues to vomit liquid; sometimes he starts vomiting liquid. *Vomiting of liquid is the most serious symptom a cat can have.* In gastro-enteritis there is also an intestinal upset and diarrhea is usually present, the bowel movements having a characteristic, unpleasant odor.

Experienced people are so quick in detecting the symptoms of gastritis and gastro-enteritis that they start treatment almost before these actually appear; undoubtedly, many cases are checked before they have an opportunity to get started.

You should know just what dosage of milk of magnesia your cat requires, and don't try to put it all down at once, as it will never be retained in that way. Warm it, and administer in small amounts with a teaspoon or medicine dropper. Even with these precautions the cat may not retain it. If the cat has been constipated it is most important that the bowels move, and an enema may be given. (The method of administering an enema is discussed in the section on Constipation.)

A case of gastritis or gastro-enteritis can be properly handled only when the cat is confined to a cage.

Inoculations are now part of the treatment of these diseases.

Important. Don't permit a high irrigation.

Allowing a cat to vomit liquid for any length of time, without taking measures to check it, is usually equivalent to killing him.

Feeding a cat that has gastritis is likewise equivalent to killing him. Any food or water taken into the stomach at such a time acts merely as an irritant. A cat can go many days without food. No food is given until the cat begins to recover; this difficult and dangerous period must be handled by the veterinarian; successfully getting the cat back to normal eating is one of the most difficult and delicate things one is called upon to do for cats—one mistake means a relapse and probable death. (*See section on Convalescent Feeding.*)

When a cat does not have gastritis. When one is worried about a cat it is comforting to know that if he purrs, stretches, yawns, and sleeps stretched out on his side, he does *not* have gastritis.

2

HEAD AND CHEST INFECTIONS

These are not diseases which happen with the suddenness of gastritis and gastro-enteritis.

When there are a heavy discharge from the eyes and nasal passages, difficulty in breathing, and difficulty in swallowing and eating, your cat is in a serious condition and your veterinarian should attend him.

VI. CARE AT HOME

HOME treatment consists of keeping a cat well. Sick cats require the attention of a competent cat veterinarian, *at once.*

Home doctoring is unwise; it is usually unsuccessful because home diagnosis is usually wrong.

The practice of calling in a veterinarian only after home methods have proved unsuccessful is unfair to the veterinarian and to the cat. Since one of the important factors in the care of a cat is to take the proper measures *as soon* as he becomes ill, waiting until he is very sick before calling the doctor is just calling the doctor to attend a hopeless case.

Careful people have their veterinarians see their cats once or twice a year. If your veterinarian is thoroughly familiar with your cat and his history, much valuable time can be saved in an emergency. When the cat falls ill you telephone the veterinarian at once; knowing all about your cat, he can promptly advise you regarding the first steps to take; thus you can start treatment even before the doctor arrives. Such quick action may mean the life of the cat.

A healthy cat. The coat of a healthy cat fairly glows; his body is hard and muscular. A healthy cat is active, graceful, alert, happy, sweet tempered; his eyes are clear and bright, his breath sweet. He is ready for each meal and eats with relish.

A cat in poor condition. If a cat is below par or in poor health, one notices it first in his eyes; they may be dull, red-rimmed, or watery; the third eyelid may appear over the corner of the eyes. Discharge from the eyes and nose may be a chronic condition, resulting from a serious illness, or it may result from vitamin deficiency. Hair off around the eyes indicates the cat is not well, or has been ill; it may indicate something wrong or lacking in his feeding or care. White hairs appear in the mask and around the eyes of a Siamese when he has a cold; in a serious illness his entire mask may become light. (This also may happen during the spring and summer shedding period.)

Inactive, dull and cross cats are usually in poor condition. They are frequently stiff and awkward in the handling of their bodies. Offensive breath and excessive thinness usually indicate something not quite right.

Spiky fur—when the fur stands up in bunches—always indicates a cat does not feel well. Dull, rough, or uneven coat, as well as excessive shedding, indicates a cat in poor condition.

Building up a cat that is below par. It is wisest to consult your veterinarian to try to discover why your cat is not in perfect condition. Much time may be saved by having a competent person tell you just where the trouble is.

Certainly a good tonic is always in order; it must be given over a period of time in order to get results. As any remedy loses some of its effectiveness when constantly used, tonics are best when used for a few weeks and then discontinued for a week or two; repeat until the cat is definitely improved. Do not give tonic to an overfed cat. Give a corrective laxative and stop feeding so much.

It must be remembered that cats do badly or even become ill from loneliness, unhappiness, fright, or the loss of a human or cat companion.

1

EYE CONDITIONS AND VITAMIN A DEFICIENCY

Eye conditions are often secondary; for this reason the eyes should be kept clean with warm, saturated borax solution while the primary cause is being found and cured. Argyrol and other things used in the eyes should be prescribed by the veterinarian. The tiny bit of dried matter which is found in the corners of the eyes after sleeping should just be removed; this does not call for bathing of the eyes. Red-rimmed eyes and even eyes with a heavy discharge are sometimes the result of Vitamin A deficiency.

Vitamin A deficiency. Serious lack of Vitamin A results in decreased resistance to infection of the eyes, the mucous membranes of the respiratory tract, and the glands, and predisposes to distemper. More than fifty per cent of experimental animals with Vitamin A deficiency develop urinary stones.

Recent biological studies have shown that cats are unable to transform and make use of carotene, the natural form of Vitamin A. Carotene is present in most leafy vegetables, milk, butter, and egg yolk. Ordinarily, the carotene in these things is changed in the liver to Vitamin A; this change does not occur in cats. Cats may be particularly liable to Vitamin A deficiency.

To supply the vitamin needs of the average cat, Dr. Camuti has prepared a liquid vitamin tonic, which has been entirely successful. It is usually given in the food.

Halibut liver and other fish liver oil concentrates are a good source of the essential Vitamin A. Cod liver oil, to be effective, must be administered in such quantities that it may upset the digestive balance and, therefore, it is inadvisable to use it.

2

RICKETS AND CALCIUM DEFICIENCY

Rickets is a softening of the bones due to calcium deficiency; it is a common danger to all breeds of kittens, and may appear at any time up to six months of age.

The kitten may go suddenly and completely lame, or just limp slightly after jumping from some high place, or when some other cat plays roughly with him. Normal kittens fall fifty times a day and are never injured; nor are they injured by their mothers or other cats, no matter how roughly they may play with them.

Before lameness is apparent it is possible to detect a lack of development in the rear quarters and a lack of flexibility in the movements of the body; usually the kitten will have an abnormally large abdomen and appear to be fat; he is pudgy rather than lithe and slim.

Many people who sell kittens young and do not keep track of them in their new homes never know that their kittens are developing rickets after leaving them.

Under-nourished mother cats are very likely to produce kittens that will have rickets, particularly in later life, after all reserve of calcium has been taken from their own bodies. Even if a mother cat is capable of producing kittens without rickets, it is unwise and unkind to place such a strain upon her; for her own good, as well as that of her kittens, she should have the support and help of extra calcium and vitamins in the latter part of the gestation period and during the lactation period.

Cure for rickets. If a kitten has definitely developed rickets, a good cat veterinarian will be required to handle the case. Inoculations are effective, but expensive; it is much cheaper to take measures to prevent rickets, particularly as the things given to kittens to prevent this condition also assure proper development and growth, good bone formation, sound teeth, and resistance against disease.

A kitten that has had rickets badly, although cured, will never quite have the straight legs and trim lines of a normal cat.

A cat being treated for rickets requires a cage, as he must be prevented from much jumping.

Prevention of rickets. Calcium must be fed to the mother cat, and to the kittens up to the seventh month, when their second teeth are in. This must be a form of calcium or compound of calciums which cats can assimilate; cats are unable to assimilate some forms. Dr. Camuti's calcium wafers for cats are compounded of those forms of calcium best suited to cats, and have a hundred per cent record of success when fed according to directions.

Unfortunately, the administering of calcium is complicated by the fact that it is not properly assimilated except in conjunction with Vitamin D. Dr. Camuti's liquid vitamin tonic, mentioned in the preceding section on Vitamin A deficiency, is also a safe source of Vitamin D. Halibut liver oil *with Viosterol* and similar concentrates, such as Squibb Navitol, furnish Vitamin D as well as Vitamin A. They should be used in dosages only as prescribed by a veterinarian. Cod liver oil, as before stated, is unsatisfactory. Plain halibut liver oil *without Viosterol* does not contain Vitamin D in effective quantities.

Warning. Never use a concentrated form of Vitamin D *without* calcium. This induces a condition resembling rickets; kittens fed Vitamin D without calcium go down on their rear quarters.

3

TEETH

At the same time you are supplying your kitten with calcium to prevent rickets you are providing him with a fine set of teeth.

A cat's food is mostly soft, and bones are dangerous for cats. Kibbled food is a safe hard food which most cats like; this does give them something to chew.

You should examine your cat's teeth frequently. If he is gentle you can clean his teeth with peroxide, or just with a dry swab. Most cats are very difficult when you try to do anything with their teeth. When a cat's teeth are discolored he should go to his veterinarian to have them cleaned; while cleaning them the veterinarian will discover any decayed teeth which should be removed. Just like human beings, cats suffer many ill effects from a head full of bad teeth. They are much better out. Many cats that have had all their teeth removed at a comparatively early age have managed quite nicely on soft foods and liquids.

4

EARS

A cat's ears should be clean. If dust and wax accumulate in the outer ear this can be wiped out with a dry soft cloth or a dry cotton swab. If a cat's ears are healthy there is no reason for putting anything into them; anything thus inserted acts as an irritant.

Neglected cats and stray cats usually have ear mites. It is impossible to see ear mites except under a microscope; however, when they are present the inner ear canal is full of dark granular matter; as the condition gets worse the cat may carry his head to one side or shake it, and he may scratch the back of his ears until he injures the skin. An irritation sometimes appears on the face near the ears.

If a mother cat has ear mites her kittens will also have them.

Of all the parasites common to cats, ear mites are the greatest nuisance. They can be cured and it can be done at home, but one must have great patience, for the treatment, as a rule, extends over many months. If the mites are not completely eliminated the trouble will, of course, start all over again.

The medicine used to kill ear mites must penetrate to the innermost parts of the ears; for this purpose oil is more effective than ointment or powder. Dr. Camuti's antiseptic oil is recommended.

If a clean cat, free from ear mites, must live with one that is being treated for mites, oil should be kept in the ears of both cats.

Serious disorders of the ear require the attention of a good veterinarian.

5

FLEAS

Cats, no matter how sheltered, may sometimes get fleas. This is no disgrace. The disgrace lies in not getting rid of them instantly.

House cats seldom get fleas. If a flea comb is run through their fur once a week, the first fleas to appear will be eliminated and no bad infestation need be feared.

Cats badly infested with fleas can be treated safely with a good flea powder *made for cats.* Do not apply near the time of a meal.

Cats constantly exposed to fleas, such as those running out of doors in the grass, must be dusted weekly with powder. Their bedding should be changed frequently.

If a mother cat has fleas her kittens will have fleas.

6

WORMS

There are two common types of worms, round worm and tape worm. There is a safe remedy for round worm and another for tape worm.

Do not worm your cat or kitten on general principles nor give him worm medicine as a conditioner. There is no reason to believe that a medicine designed to kill worms should act as a tonic for a cat. It is quite true that the laxative effect of some worm medicines may have beneficial results, and the cat appear in much better health after the worming. But when a cat needs a laxative it is much easier on the cat, and safer, to use a proper laxative.

Worm your cat for the kind of worms he has. Sometimes worms are vomited or discovered in the stool. If you do not recognize the kind, your veterinarian can advise you.

If for any reason you think that your cat may have worms, have a specimen of the stool analyzed to determine whether he has.

It is a common mistake to suspect worms every time a cat behaves in any way not quite normal. *Don't make this mistake.* If you have purchased a clean, healthy kitten, from a reliable person, there is no reason to imagine he has worms, unless you yourself have exposed him to them. Of course, if a mother cat has worms her kittens will also have them.

Street cats, stray cats, and all cats that run out of doors cannot help getting worms, eventually. Cats that run out can be wormed once or twice a year. Breeders of cats who are continually bringing in new stock must worm at regular intervals, unless each new cat is isolated and wormed before introduction into the cattery.

Once you have completely eliminated worms from all your cats there is no reason for their having them again unless they are exposed. A successful worming means that the cat has no opportunity to reinfest himself from sanitary pan or bedding. A cage is a convenient place for worming.

Those who have more than one cat may just as well worm them all at one time, as cats living together infest each other.

Worming. If you can administer tablets, and know where to get remedies absolutely safe for cats, you can worm your own cats.

Never worm a sick cat. It frequently happens that a sick cat vomits worms, and the owner concludes he is sick because he has worms; worm medicine administered at such a time may kill the cat. A cat that has worms badly enough to vomit them has had them a long time and can wait for worming until he is feeling well again. Vomiting is a symptom of gastritis or a gastric upset; anything as strong as worm medicine, administered at such a time, is almost sure to be fatal.

Cats subject to chronic constipation are difficult to worm; such cats usually require a laxative before and after worming; it should be a non-irritating laxative, such as milk of magnesia.

Kittens may be wormed at three months of age, if they are well.

If a cat has both tape and round worms, at least two weeks should be allowed to elapse between wormings.

7

HAIR BALL

Every time a cat washes himself he swallows hair, and a cat washes himself a great deal. Every effort must be made to eliminate as much loose hair as possible by grooming. Provision must also be made to aid the cat in passing the hair he swallows; otherwise a hair ball forms in the stomach or intestines. In neglected cats it gets so large that it cannot be passed and eventually kills the cat. A hair ball is a hard mass of hair, which may be round or long.

Even well-groomed Short-Hairs will sometimes get hair balls. Every possible means must constantly be employed to prevent this great danger to cats.

Extra care must be given during shedding periods. Cats in poor condition shed excessively; cats may shed badly after an illness or after a change from country to city. All cats shed in the spring.

In the wild state cats shed loose hair in brushing through undergrowth; it is also blown away by the wind. We use a brush and comb for this purpose, which really should be much more effective. A thorough daily grooming is imperative.

In the wild state cats eat grass, which causes them to

vomit swallowed hair. House cats crave grass, and it can be grown for them to prevent their eating potted plants, cut flowers, artificial flowers, broom straws, and all such things which attract them. Grain seed grows readily in the house and cats like it. It is important to note that grass is given to cats to satisfy their craving for it and to cause them to vomit hair; *never* as a first aid measure when a cat is ill; a cat that is ill or coming down with an illness should never have grass. Vomiting is present in gastritis, the most deadly of cat diseases; it can readily be seen that causing a cat to vomit if he is coming down with gastritis is absolutely wrong and extremely dangerous.

We have one more weapon against hair ball—lubricants. White vaseline and mineral oil have long been used to help carry off swallowed hair. There is now a more effective lubricant which is also highly successful in breaking down hair balls which have formed; this is Laxamel, a product of Burroughs Wellcome & Co. Laxamel contains malt, which is beneficial to the coat.

Important. Do not mix a lubricant with food. This makes it less effective in eliminating hair and also coats the food, thus depriving the cat of his proper nourishment.

Preventing hair ball. As discussed above, effective grooming, fresh growing grain, and a lubricant, are the three ways of combating the danger of hair ball.

As a preventive, a lubricant may be administered weekly, the maximum dose being about one teaspoonful; do not give enough to cause diarrhea. During shedding periods a lubricant may be given daily; naturally, the dosage would have to be a little smaller. Laxamel can be given with a teaspoon or can be taken in the fingers and dropped into the back of the mouth; the head is held up and the mouth almost closed, until it is swallowed. If a cat is receiving a teaspoonful to a dose, he cannot swallow more than half a teaspoonful at one time.

Cats soon learn to like Laxamel and white vaseline and eat them voluntarily. If a cat is particularly difficult to handle, vaseline can be smeared over his paws; he will wash it off.

Symptoms of hair ball. A dry cough, frequent vomiting of meals just after they are eaten, and intermittent constipation or complete stoppage of the bowels are the most frequent symptoms of hair ball.

Treatment to eliminate hair ball. If there is complete stoppage of the bowels, your veterinarian must see the cat at once. Otherwise, you may try to break down the hair ball by administering a lubricant every day until the symptoms which alarmed you have disappeared. Laxamel is recommended for breaking down hair balls. The dosage must be regulated by the tolerance of the cat; administer daily in as great amount as possible without causing diarrhea. Examination of the feces will reveal how much hair is being eliminated. Treatment may extend over many weeks. If you do not notice some improvement in two or three weeks, put the case in the hands of your veterinarian.

8

CONSTIPATION

A cat or kitten should have a daily well-formed movement. If the cat is healthy and properly fed, the odor is not offensive. There is no cause for alarm if a grown cat has not more than six movements in a week, provided his health is good and he is not toxic.

Naturally, the wise person wishes to find the cause of constipation and eliminate it. Just dosing a cat with laxatives will ward off trouble only for a time; medicines which are used constantly lose their effectiveness; cats treated in such a way will become toxic eventually.

The most common causes of constipation are incorrect diet, an accumulation of hair or a hair ball, an inherent tendency, and lack of exercise. The diet can be corrected by adding laxative foods; the swallowed hair can be eliminated with lubricants; cats with an inherited tendency will require a larger proportion of laxative foods; interesting playthings and an active young cat companion will stimulate a lazy cat to take exercise.

Overfed cats can be kept in reasonably good health by the frequent use of laxatives, but this kind of care is not recommended. Overfeeding is not a kindness to any cat.

Red-rimmed eyes may indicate a laxative is needed.

Laxative foods. Dry prepared cat foods, non-starchy vegetables, milk, and liver are laxative.

Kinds of laxatives. (1) Milk of magnesia. For a quick, safe cleaning out, the liquid form of milk of magnesia is unequaled. It is very important to know that when a cat starts to get ill, no matter what the sickness is, milk of magnesia is administered at once. It is even given as a first step in the treatment of diarrhea. The amount given as a dose cannot be exactly stated, as it depends upon the individual response. Kittens from three to nine months of age get from one-half to one teaspoonful; grown cats, from one to three teaspoonfuls. It is extremely wise to find out what your cat requires for a dose; do so before he becomes ill, as then is hardly the time to experiment.

A cat cannot swallow more than half a teaspoonful of liquid at one time. In cases of a gastric upset (and we never know how close a cat is to that) a large amount of cold liquid taken into the stomach at one time will not be retained. It is advisable to warm the liquid and give slowly with a teaspoon or medicine dropper.

(2) Lubricants. Laxamel, mineral oil, and white vaseline are lubricants. They are used to carry off hair and in emergencies when a cat has eaten splintered bones, broom straws, or any such sharp objects; also when string and textile material have been eaten.

(3) Tablets. A corrective laxative made for cats is excellent for occasional constipation and in treating chronic constipation.

Important. Don't use drastic laxatives such as castor oil or tablets intended for human beings.

Enemas. It is not surprising that a cat's intestines are just as delicate as the rest of his body. High irrigations are too severe for a cat in good health; they are usually fatal to a sick cat. Veterinarians who are cat specialists understand giving irrigations to cats; they are frequently necessary when there is complete stoppage of the bowels.

Enemas can safely and easily be given at home. An ear syringe with soft rubber tip is suitable for kittens and grown cats. A warm solution of salt or bicarbonate of soda may be used. One bulbful is usually sufficient for a small kitten, two or three for a grown cat. *Take plenty of time and use no force.*

Sometimes after a journey or in a new home a cat may not use his pan for several days. It may be that laxatives are not retained, or that the owner does not wish to risk upsetting the cat's stomach with a laxative;

an enema will safely move the bowels and the cat will also urinate.

If a cat goes frequently to his pan, strains, and is unable to urinate, his veterinarian must see him at once.

9

INFECTIONS

When a cat is injured, particularly when he is scratched or bitten by another animal, something should be applied to the injury. Dr. Camuti's antiseptic oil promotes the proper healing of a wound.

As few cats will tolerate a bandage, it is advisable when external applications are used, to hold the cat at least ten or fifteen minutes, so that the medicine will have some time to penetrate before the cat washes it off.

Infections of cats, like those of human beings, can be treated with wet dressings of epsom salt solution; the proportion is one tablespoonful dissolved in one cup of hot water. If the infected part happens to be a paw or tail the matter is less difficult, as the part can be immersed in the solution and held there for thirty minutes several times a day. (Male cats sometimes get an infected condition of the tail.) This treatment will usually cause any matter which may be present to localize, and usually it will drain almost without aid; after soaking, just cleanse with cotton, dry, apply antiseptic oil, and hold the cat as long as possible for the oil to be absorbed, unless a bandage is being used.

Holding a wet dressing over an infected part is rather difficult; it must be done for as long periods as the cat will tolerate.

Local infections which do not drain with the above treatment must be lanced by the veterinarian.

Unless you have had considerable experience with infections it is best to let your veterinarian handle them for you.

10

COLDS

A dry cough, accompanied by no symptoms of a cold, usually indicates an accumulation of hair in the throat, a hair ball, or indigestion.

If a cat sneezes once or twice, and there are no symptoms of a cold, the probability is that he has a hair or dust in his nose. Cats and kittens in new homes frequently sneeze a great deal from dust, owing to all the investigating they must do. Warm, dry air in city apartments may cause sneezing.

When a cat starts to catch cold he should be placed immediately in his cage, and kept there at an even temperature until he is well. A dose of milk of magnesia and light feeding may check the cold without recourse to medicines. If not, your veterinarian will supply the proper medicine.

Don't neglect a cold. Build the cat up with a tonic afterward; sore eyes and chronic sniffles may be the result of neglect at such a time.

No small animal should sleep on the floor; there may be a draught at any time of the year. Cat beds made of wood give proper protection; short-haired cats prefer the covered type. Cats that refuse to sleep in a bed on the floor may accept it if it is placed on a table or some high place. Siamese prefer a small, snug bed.

Some people permit their cats to sleep with them at night. Kittens are restless, and it is difficult to manage them and keep them in a suitable place. Grown cats can be taught, in very cold weather, to sleep with head and shoulders out, just like a person. Ordinarily a cat will sleep at the foot of the bed, and no draught should blow over him. Cats positively must not be permitted to sleep completely under the covers, get too warm, and then get out to lie in a draught or sit in a cold window.

11

VOMITING

Vomiting in cats presents a real problem; some cats vomit frequently. Sometimes it means nothing at all; sometimes it means that most deadly of all things—gastritis.

People experienced in the handling of cats are usually able to determine why a cat vomited and whether it was serious. Such people always have on hand a nausea tablet, which can safely be given no matter what the cause of vomiting; it should not be thought of as a medicine; it is just something to soothe the stomach. If your veterinarian has not supplied you with such a tablet, get a vial of Dr. Camuti's nausea tablets.

A cat sometimes loses a meal just after he has eaten it. This may be because he ate too fast, or because the food was too cold or too rich; a hair ball or nervousness may be the cause. If a cat has had nothing to eat for a very long time a small meal should be given, as he would probably lose a large one.

If a cat is active and playful and healthy just before and after losing a meal—if he purrs and stretches and runs and leaps—the chances are you are not going to have any trouble. A tablet will soothe his stomach; take his grass away and make his next regular meal a small and simple one.

Vomiting hair, grass, or both, is natural and should not worry you unless the cat begins to vomit liquid or seems ill.

Losing a meal hours after it has been eaten and vomiting liquid are the most serious things which can happen to a cat. This is discussed in the section on Gastritis.

Unless you are *absolutely sure* that vomiting has no serious cause, proceed exactly as in cases of gastritis. Nothing will be lost by this; you have everything to gain; in this way many potential cases of gastritis are checked.

Important. Never coax a cat to eat when he refuses his regular food. Rather, take away all food and water, and give milk of magnesia. If he vomits, give nausea tablets. Even if nothing serious develops, follow rules for convalescent feeding; a relapse or a second upset is always more serious than the first.

12

DIARRHEA

There are two types of diarrhea, the serious kind present in many diseases, and the simple kind due to natural causes, such as improper feeding, etc.

When diarrhea is present in serious diseases, the odor is characteristically offensive and easily detected by an experienced person. The doctor should be called at once.

Simple diarrhea must be checked promptly, as it is depleting and may lead to more serious trouble. There is medicine to check diarrhea, but this will be of little use unless the cause is found and remedied.

Administering milk of magnesia is the first step in the treatment of diarrhea.

Possible causes of simple diarrhea: stale food, wrong food, too much laxative food, such as milk and liver, icy cold food, bones, food fed in chunks or pieces, abrupt change in diet.

If milk is too laxative for a cat, lime water may be added in the proportion of one teaspoonful to a cup of milk. Bringing the milk to a boil also cuts down the laxative effect.

If an irritated condition of the intestines causes chronic diarrhea or an unpleasant odor, an intestinal antiseptic may be necessary. Your veterinarian will prescribe this.

13

TOXIC CONDITION

A toxic condition results from overfeeding, wrong feeding, constipation, and lack of activity; it cuts down a cat's resistance to disease.

A cat in good condition can come in contact with germs or eat stale or tainted food, and survive. He may be strong enough to throw off germs or the ill effects of things usually dangerous to cats.

A toxic cat, on the other hand, not only has no resistance to disease, but may actually fall ill of the poisons with which his system is filled.

Bad breath, rough and dull fur, excessive shedding, no hair on the ears, skin disorders, strong and offensive body odor, offensive odor from the sanitary pan, twitching of the skin, frequent colds, chronic sniffles, red-rimmed and watery eyes, uncertain temper, and lack of playfulness are some of the indications of a toxic condition.

A change to the simple diet suggested in this book, together with a course of a corrective laxative, has quickly cured many cases of twitching skin.

14

SKIN DISORDERS

The weekly inspection with the flea comb promptly reveals the beginning of any skin trouble.

Sometimes a cat may have a bare spot for no apparent reason and with no serious consequences. Usually, skin conditions are either parasitic or can be traced to diet.

Skin disorders due to improper feeding. The various forms of eczema, from the dry dandruff-like condition along the back to the more serious forms, are due to wrong food, too rich food, too much starchy food, or overfeeding. Feeding an exclusive diet of tinned food is one of the quickest ways of giving a cat eczema. There is no point in treating eczema externally unless the cause is found and remedied. Once a cat has had eczema, it may return annually in a mild form. Dry skin is undoubtedly aggravated by steam heat and warm dry air.

Parasitic skin disorders. Only a veterinarian can tell you what kind of skin disorder your cat has. Some types of parasitic skin disorders may be contracted by people. Strange cats should never be handled; when a new cat with unknown history is acquired he should be isolated for a safe period of time.

Treatment. Giving milk of magnesia is the first step.

Skin disorders require external treatment, presenting one of the most serious problems in the handling of cats; this treatment should be undertaken at home, under your veterinarian's supervision.

The odor of some medicines makes cats salivate; this is not dangerous, provided the salivation is not excessive and the medicine is a *proven remedy for cats.* Nothing is more important than consulting a veterinarian who knows cats and who will not use dog remedies on your cat.

Cats will seldom keep on bandages; in certain cases a ruff about the neck will protect the infected parts. If possible, a cat immediately washes off anything that is applied. Some clever people have contrived pajamas which the cats could not get off. In most cases the only way to get a cat to leave medicine on long enough for it to do any good is to hold him. You will get a lot of reading done while treating a case of skin trouble! It is sometimes possible to play with a cat and divert his attention during treatment.

15

INVALIDS AND CONVALESCENTS

Sick cats require quiet and protection from draughts and bright light, and they must be kept under constant observation. All of these things are possible only when the cat is in a cage.

After serious operations, such as spaying, cats must be treated as invalids; they must be carefully handled and fed until they are back to normal. After any gastric upset, no matter how trivial, care must be taken in feeding. After slight upsets, start feeding when the cat appears hungry and asks for food.

Invalid food. Concentrated beef broth, made at home, and with all fat removed, is probably the most suitable invalid food. If a cat is accustomed to milk, he may retain that. Dr. Camuti's liquid vitamin tonic mixed with broth or milk has kept many cats alive and aided in their recovery.

Convalescent food. The change from liquids to solids must be very gradual. If an invalid is getting a teaspoonful of broth every two hours, it will be many days before his stomach will accept solid food. As cooked beef seems more readily retained by a sick cat, a little can be fed finely minced and mixed with broth, as the first step toward solid food. After cooked beef is being taken well, feeding raw scraped beef is usually the next step. Of course, meals are very small and at frequent intervals. Keep to plain unmixed foods for many days. *Avoid fish.*

The point is that an empty stomach will not retain solid food, nor much liquid at one time. Great caution is required in convalescent feeding. Even after only a slight upset, care must be exercised.

After a long fast a cat may have no desire to eat; much coaxing and feeding with a medicine dropper may be necessary. A vitamin tonic is excellent in such cases, as it builds up the cat and, at the same time, stimulates his appetite.

Cats with bad colds are sometimes fed by hand when they cannot smell food and, therefore, have no urge to eat.

Dainty eaters may be stimulated to an interest in food by the presence of other cats eating.

16

ADMINISTERING MEDICINES

With the cat's sensitive stomach, tendency to gastritis, and inability to tolerate certain drugs, it is essential that only *tested cat remedies* be given to your cat.

It cannot be repeated too often that dog remedies and human remedies must be avoided. Certain drugs considered mild and safe for babies and for dogs can kill a cat in five minutes. Even when not poisonous to cats, remedies that are too strong may cause violent nausea and lead to gastritis.

Cats salivate from fear, because they dislike the taste or smell of a medicine and because some medicine is too strong. Medicine too strong for a cat must not be administered. Slight salivation from fear or dislike of a medicine is not serious.

A cat is the most difficult of patients; he is timid, frightened, perverse. Unless handled with utmost tact he may get to fear the person treating him. Every effort must be made to retain the confidence of your cat.

Cats should be accustomed from kittenhood to taking tablets; then they will be easy to handle. Every cat owner should learn to give tablets quickly and expertly without wrapping a cat or using force in any way. It is merely a matter of opening the mouth and popping in the tablet before the cat knows what has happened. A small tablet placed well back in the center of the throat is swallowed naturally as you close the cat's mouth and stroke his throat. If you have a cat that doesn't mind lying on his back in your lap you may be able to drop a tablet into his throat while he is lying in that position.

If the tablet is large it must be poked into the throat; this takes considerable skill, as it is a very serious thing to be bitten.

The cat's claws should always be clipped.

No two cats respond in quite the same way; the problem is between you and your cat. With someone to help you, it is quite easy; with the cat in a sitting position, your helper can place a hand back of him to pre-

Photograph by Mina Turner

BLUE POINT SIAMESE

vent his backing up and can hold his front feet in position with the other hand. This leaves your two hands free to administer the medicine, and there is no danger of interference from the front feet. In working alone, it sometimes helps to pin a heavy blanket around the cat's neck, just to obstruct his front feet. Wrapping a cat completely in a blanket causes him to struggle; it may terrify him badly. An expert shouldn't have to wrap her own cat.

Cats are capable of holding tablets in their mouths and then spitting them out later. Watch for this.

Liquids are really more difficult to give than tablets; when a tablet is down, it is down; liquid may be all over the cat. A grown cat cannot swallow more than half a teaspoonful at a time, a kitten much less. Because of cats' sensitive stomachs, all liquids should be at room temperature or warmer. Taking plenty of time, give the required dosage in small amounts with a teaspoon or small medicine dropper; inserted into the mouth, the spoon keeps it open while the liquid is poured in; the medicine dropper can usually be inserted at the side of the mouth, if you are careful and use a small one.

Very few medicines should be given near meal-time or with a meal. A cat's distaste for medicine may upset him to the extent of losing the meal; while this may do him no harm, it is not good for him. Tonics, calcium, and vitamin concentrates may be given in food. Most medicines should be given as far between meals as possible; the same is true of flea powder and all external applications. Do not mix lubricants with food.

Never forget that getting medicine which cats can retain has been the great problem in their treatment. Between their fear and their sensitive stomachs they present a constant problem.

17

SPECIAL PROBLEMS

The special problem of long-haired cats is hair ball. They swallow more hair in cleaning themselves; therefore, greater care must be taken in preventing hair ball. This breed sometimes suffers during extremely hot weather. At such times they should be kept quiet and as cool as possible without subjecting them to draughts; light food and not much of it is called for; no heavy oils.

Siamese cats are the latest breed imported in any great number to this country; they were confronted here with extreme differences in climate and methods of feeding. While it can be said that Siamese cats are now thoroughly acclimated, they have their peculiar traits. They like heat more than any other breed. It is not advisable to pamper them nor to keep apartments warmer because of them; but they should have snug beds of their own (the covered wooden beds are best), where they may curl up to sleep when they find the apartment too cool for their tastes. Siamese particularly should not be subjected to extremes in temperature. They travel best in small carriers having ventilation at one end only.

Siamese cats have even more sensitive stomachs than other breeds, which makes it very important what medicine is given to them. Special care should be exercised in worming them; do it at home and use only worm medicine proven safe for Siamese cats.

VII. ACQUIRING A NEW CAT OR KITTEN

KITTENS adapt themselves to new homes more readily than grown cats. The younger a cat is the less upset he is by any change.

Kittens are capable of adapting themselves to new surroundings, and they can be trained and taught to fit properly into a household. Grown cats are very set in their ways; to a large extent, they force people to do the adjusting.

Getting two kittens at one time is wise and very kind; they grow up happily and normally together, providing endless joy and amusement. In many ways, two cats are more easily cared for than one.

When the cats in a household number three or more, even if they are all altered cats, clashes of temperament are likely. Squabbles between altered cats are seldom serious, but they should not be allowed to occur.

Choice of cats. People have a decided tendency to acquire cat after cat of the same breed and color. The more adventurous people, who try something new each time, learn many delightful things about the differences in breeds and types of cats.

It is quite common to hear someone say, "I hate Persians" or "I hate Siamese," when the remark is based upon no real knowledge of the breed in question. People frequently accept someone's else opinion, or judge by some unpleasant cat they may have encountered, not stopping to realize that an unpleasant cat is probably a mismanaged cat. Such conclusions are very, very unfair to all the lovely and satisfactory cats of all breeds which we may acquire for pets.

Exquisite color combinations and contrasts in temperament are possible, and productive of endless pleasure to the discriminating owner.

1

INTRODUCING A CAT OR KITTEN INTO A NEW HOME

If the new cat is past the kitten age, use discretion in handling him until you know just how reliable he is and what he likes. Extremely nervous grown cats may appear to enjoy being stroked one moment and spring at you the next.

In most cases people acquire a kitten. The first two weeks in his new home are the most important of his life; much depends upon how these two weeks are managed.

The adjustment period is longer for a grown cat than for a kitten. During this period the good of the cat must be the first consideration; he positively must not be thought of as a new toy to enjoy and to show off—there will be many years ahead for this pleasant diversion.

Whether or not a cat appears to be frightened, he really is upset by the change into a new home. He must be shielded from excitement and confusion. Let him get acquainted with one room and one person first. If you have a cage, he may be happier there.

If a new cat hisses or growls, do not conclude he is cross or has a bad disposition. A cat hisses and growls because he is frightened; he also runs away and hides when he is frightened; he may just crouch in a corner. The arched back and hair on end, on the contrary, is really a game which a cat usually enjoys; when he is adjusted in his new home your cat will probably appreciate your helping him play this game.

After any exhausting experience a cat will sleep a great deal. For this reason cats sometimes sleep a lot soon after going into a new home; or they may show great animation for several days, and then proceed to sleep almost continually.

You should take your new cat or kitten at some time when you can devote several days to him. If you can leave your carrier for him to play around for a day or two in his old home, he will not be so frightened when taken out in it, and he will have at least one thing in his new home which is not absolutely strange to him. He may like to sleep in it.

A cat or kitten that has lived with other cats, and particularly a kitten that has never been away from his mother and brothers and sisters, will be desperately lonely in strange surroundings, with strange people, and without the comfort of his mother and his cat companions. For this reason he may cry a great deal; just be patient until your love and devotion have made him forget his loneliness. Do not be discouraged if his crying continues for a week; he has many adjustments to make. He should not, however, cry when you are with him, or at least not when you are devoting your attention to him; if he does, he is probably a noisy cat.

Health. A cat or kitten needs to be absolutely healthy in order to stand up under the strain of changing to a new home; new owners should try not to add to this strain by improper handling. His feeding must be right; he must use his pan; he must have plenty of sleep; he must be kept in an even temperature.

A feeding schedule is always provided with the kitten. Do not feed for several hours, until his first nervousness is over. Make no changes in feeding and feed lightly for a few days. If the previous feeding was wrong, don't try to make a complete change in less than two or three weeks.

If you know nothing of how the cat was fed previously, feed ground raw or cooked beef and give him milk between meals. If he refuses this for a day or two and you have reason to believe his refusal is not from nervousness or sickness, you may have to try him with other foods in order to find something he will take before he has fasted too long.

If a new cat or kitten refuses food you know he is accustomed to, do not try to coax him with something else; offer him food at intervals until he is ready to eat. If he is nervous or sick he should not eat.

Cats are always constipated after a change. If a small amount of lubricant is given the day before he makes the change, and a little each day thereafter, it is possible that normal movements will be maintained. (See section on Constipation.)

If your new cat has diarrhea the first day you get him, the previous owner is to blame. If he seems well in every other way, you may be safe in trying to correct the condition yourself; give milk of magnesia and put the cat on a straight beef diet. If this does not correct the condition in one or two days, and particularly if there is an offensive odor, you had better have your veterinarian advise you promptly.

Sleeping arrangements. Giving a new cat or kitten complete liberty in his new home, either night or day, is inviting trouble. He will sharpen his claws in the wrong place, he will forget where his pan is and, if he sleeps at all, he may sleep in a draught.

Many people permit their grown cats to sleep with them; kittens are too restless and are sure to get out and sleep in a draught or get into mischief.

A cage or some small room, such as the bathroom, is suitable. The new kitten should be placed there the first night and no attention paid to him if he cries; in a few nights he will accept the schedule.

Taking a young kitten during the fall or winter means extra care to be sure he sleeps in a warm and sheltered bed during the cold months.

A new cat, and particularly a new kitten, must have opportunity to sleep during the day. He can be shut away for one or two periods; he will become accustomed to the schedule and be the better for extra sleep. People getting their first Siamese may not know that he will overdo and get much too excited if he is encouraged to play and show off too long at a time.

Chewing and eating blankets and towels. Be watchful; if you find a hole in his blanket, make him sleep on paper. Keep all wool away.

The sanitary pan. Be sure the new cat or kitten knows where his pan is; *confine him to small quarters until it has been used several times.* You cannot be sure for a week or two how reliable he is; therefore, do not let him out of his cage or room except when you are with him and can watch him. Mistakes are most often made on beds and rugs and in bath tubs.

Be sure you are using the material he is accustomed to in his pan. A change can be made later if you wish it; first, mix the two materials and then gradually eliminate the one you do not care to use.

Don't imagine a cat does not require watching just because he is grown; any cat, no matter how old or how well trained, may make a mistake in a new home.

It is up to you to see that such a mistake has no opportunity to occur.

Claw sharpening arrangements. As in the case of his sanitary pan, the cat must have what he has been accustomed to; it must be ready and waiting for him, and it must be the first thing used in his new home. Any opportunity for him to use anything else must be avoided.

A well-mannered cat. No matter how perfect a kitten's training may have been, his new owner must continue the training, or he will develop bad habits very quickly. That is why he should be confined to small quarters whenever he cannot be watched; his introduction into rooms filled with rugs and furniture should be gradual and under supervision.

Supervision and discipline during the first six months of his life will mean a cat with nice manners—surely to the best interest of both the cat and his owner.

If you have just gotten your first Siamese, you may not know how companionable they are and how much love and attention they require. If the cat must remain alone all day, the adjustment will be difficult, unless there is a dog or another cat companion. Such a companion gives the Siamese something on which to lavish his love and a means of using up his great energy. He will still have plenty of love and affection for people.

2

INTRODUCING A CAT OR KITTEN INTO A HOME WHERE THERE IS ALREADY A CAT

Cats get along with dogs and with other cats; the introduction is easiest when the new arrival is very young.

Putting the new kitten immediately with the pets already in the house is hopelessly wrong. The newcomer should have at least several days to become accustomed to the sights and sounds and smells of his new home before he must get acquainted with other animals who will resent him.

The cat already living in the house will be resentful, but if he knows there is another cat in the house which he is not permitted to see, his natural curiosity will make him want to see the new arrival.

When the cats are finally allowed to see each other, a cage is very convenient, for they can get acquainted through the bars.

If no cage is available, placing cats in adjoining rooms for a day is wise. They will smell and hear each other and the desire to see each other will become greater and greater.

From two days to two months may be required for adjusting a new cat or kitten. Any sort of fight should be avoided.

Grown neuters or spayed females never fail to accept a new kitten, if the introduction is careful and tactful. They eventually love the kitten and become very devoted to it.

Breeding cats. Unaltered males and females are not nearly so easily handled. Two male cats cannot live together after they have matured; the more highly bred they are the harder they will fight. A male will not tolerate a neuter. Theoretically, a male should get along with a female or a spayed female; however, they dislike certain cats; when upset, they have also been known to attack the females with which they have always lived.

Females may be put with any other cats they happen to like. If after all the proper introductory measures have been taken, a female still dislikes another cat, that may be quite final as far as she is concerned.

It is sometimes necessary to separate cats that are fighting. To do so without getting bitten is difficult, as they are not responsible at such a time. Heavy gloves should be worn, but there is not always time to find them. The safest place to take hold of a cat is at the back of the neck.

Cats that have been fighting should be looked over for injuries.

3

ADOPTING STRAY CATS AND STREET WAIFS

If little or nothing is known about the history of the cat or kitten you are adopting, he should first be looked over and cleaned up by your veterinarian. This is particularly advisable if there are already other cats in the household.

The veterinarian will clean the fur, rid the cat of ear mites, fleas, and worms, and will isolate him for a period sufficient to make sure that he is not coming down with skin trouble or any serious disease. The veterinarian will advise you whether a tonic and special food are required to get the cat into good condition.

Never adopt a stray to save money; they are usually diseased and under-nourished; getting one into proper condition will cost as much as you would pay for a properly raised kitten.

4

BUYING FROM DEALERS

All dealers are not reliable. If the background and history of a kitten are unknown, the situation is exactly the same as in the case of adopting a stray. Every precaution should be taken not to bring trouble into your home.

Don't let anyone tell you that running eyes are not serious or that a patch or bare spot is the result of a scratch from another kitten. Don't let anyone persuade you to buy a kitten under three months of age.

No matter from whom you are buying, it is quite customary for you to insist that the cat or kitten be looked over by your veterinarian before you purchase it.

5

GIFTS

A healthy, well-raised, nice-mannered kitten is indeed a lovely gift, provided the person receiving the gift is permitted to choose it. Surprising someone with the gift of a kitten is usually a mistake; seldom do people receive what they really want.

Anyone who is presented with a female cat or kitten, supposedly for a pet, has every right to suspect the motives of the person making the gift. As a rule a female cat is *not a pet* unless she is spayed.

If the gift kitten has a pedigree it is delivered with him. To say that a kitten is pedigreed or has famous parents means absolutely nothing; if a kitten has a pedigree he has it with him. Be sure you get it.

6

BUYING A PEDIGREED CAT OR KITTEN

The pedigree of a cat tells what his background is, whether he is purely bred. Certain strains of cats have certain outstanding characteristics in appearance and in disposition. If you are buying a Long-Hair or a Siamese, the pedigree is of utmost importance; it is one of the things which makes a fine cat a fine cat; it is the legal and tangible proof of just how fine he is.

Unless you are well informed, show records and ribbons won at shows may be misleading; cats often win ribbons because there is no competition in their classes; almost any unaltered cat may become a champion if taken to enough shows.

Cost. No properly raised, pedigreed kitten should sell for less than fifty dollars. Even at this figure the breeder will probably not break even. There is nothing so expensive or difficult as the proper raising and training of kittens. The general public does not realize or appreciate this fact, and the constant demand for cheap kittens has discouraged and driven out of business many competent breeders.

It costs as much to raise fine cats as it does to raise fine dogs; first of all, the maintainance of the mother cat and the stud fee must be counted as part of the cost. A kitten cheaply and carelessly raised, from parents improperly fed and cared for, is not worth taking home. There are no bargains in animals. Fine breeding stock, equipment, proper food, medicines, veterinary services, and advertising are very expensive. Whole litters are sometimes lost. There is the care, the constant supervision, the training, and possibly long days and nights of nursing. How people can expect so much for less than the actual cost of feeding the mother cat and kittens is beyond understanding, but easily explains why the market is flooded with poorly raised, sickly kittens.

7

WHAT TO LOOK FOR WHEN BUYING A CAT OR KITTEN

The most important thing is to make certain that you are dealing with a reliable person of experience, whose kittens have given satisfaction as to health and as pets. A reliable breeder will insist upon keeping in touch with the kitten in his new home until he is all set and everything is running smoothly.

Health. No matter how experienced you are, you should permit your veterinarian to examine and give his approval of the cat or kitten you are purchasing. This should be done before you take it into your home.

VIII. BREEDS OF CATS

THERE are four breeds of cats commonly found in America.

1

LONG-HAIR

Today all long-haired cats are properly called Long-Hairs. Their outstanding beauty is their coats, which should be long, full, and flowing, with extra-long hair about the neck to make the beautiful ruff. The tail is full, and short enough to be in proper proportion to the cobby body; the legs are short and heavy, the head large, with small ears set well apart, and the nose short. The eyes are large and round and of copper or orange, except in the case of white cats, which may have blue or copper eyes, and the silvers, which have green eyes.

Long-haired cats are in the following colors: white, black, red, blue (maltese), cream, chinchilla, smoke, shaded silver, masked silver, silver tabby, brown tabby, red tabby, tortoise-shell.

2

DOMESTIC SHORT-HAIR

The cats casually spoken of as "alley cats" are really our domestic Short-Hair, a distinct breed. It is a mistake to consider a Short-Hair a better cat because he appears to have some Long-Hair ancestry.

The official standards require that the Short-Hair be the same cobby type as the Long-Hair. Many cat owners prefer the long, lithe panther type which we associate with the great cats of forest and jungle.

Short-haired cats are in all the colors mentioned above for Long-Hairs. White markings, while frowned upon at cat shows, are quite common and often most attractive.

3

MANX

The Manx is a short-haired cat, with very high back legs and no tail whatever. This breed is available in the colors listed above for Long-Hairs.

4

SIAMESE

The Royal and Sacred Cat of Siam comes directly from the palace in Siam, or traces his ancestry to cats of the palace or the temples, or to cats owned by royalty in Siam.

The temple and palace cats are the same in appearance. These cats are probably reverenced because the kittens are white, for white animals are held sacred in the Orient.

The kings and princes of Siam gave Siamese cats to important visitors from other lands; King Prajadhipok sent several cats back to America after his first visit here.

Many of the first palace cats to leave Siam were given to titled Englishwomen, or to people in the diplomatic service in Siam. These cats were shown in England, becoming champions, and setting the standard for Siamese cats. Some of these cats were brought to America; hundreds of their descendants are now in this country.

The real royal cat is not common in Siam, and tourists have no opportunity to secure them. Cats obtained from dealers are different in appearance and disposition.

Essentially panther-like in appearance, the royal Siamese cat is long of body, lithe, and muscular; the coat is sleek and close-lying; the rear quarters are slightly higher than the front. The tail is long, thin, and tapering; there may be a slight irregularity near the tip. The feet are trim and slender; the females are particularly dainty animals, with tiny feet and small pointed heads.

The elongated head of the Siamese cat, with slanting blue eyes, sometimes crossed, is Oriental in effect; the face is very expressive.

As a whole, Siamese are rather smaller than cats of other breeds.

There are two colorings of Siamese, designated as Seal Point and Blue Point, both characterized by dark extremities; the Seal Point has brown points—feet, tail, mask, and ears; the Blue Point has maltese points.

The Seal Point Siamese is the one most commonly seen. The shade of brown varies with age and also depends upon whether the cat comes of a light or a dark strain of cats. The body may be white, cream, fawn, tan, or even brown; dark specimens darken early and the bodies rapidly become much darker than in the case of light specimens. Siamese kittens are born white or cream in color; the points develop gradually. A kitten, therefore, does not have the full mask nor the dark body of an older cat. Siamese cats may darken and then lighten again; their shading is constantly changing. From six to twelve months of age a Siamese cat usually has the most perfect contrast between dark brown points and a clear fawn coat.

Some fine strains of Siamese cats have been bred lighter and lighter, while other fine strains have been bred darker and darker; in the light cats, the bodies are white, or nearly so, and their points lack the density of darker specimens; in the dark cats, the points are so dark as to seem black, and the bodies may be actually dark brown all over. Since both of these extremes are strains of *fine, pedigreed palace cats,* with the charming dispositions found only in these cats, it is obvious that the fineness of a Siamese cannot be judged by his coloring. A striking contrast between very dark points and a very light body does not indicate a fine Siamese cat *unless the cat also has* the important requirements of a long slender body, long head, long tail, slanting blue eyes, a sleek coat, and the aristocratic qualities of disposition characteristic of pedigreed Siamese cats.

Judging a Siamese cat by his coloring is judging him by the one thing which is constantly changing!

An unpedigreed Siamese usually has a spectacularly dark face; but with it he may have a loud voice and an unpleasant disposition. It is *breeding,* not *coloring,* which makes a fine Siamese. Gentleness, reliability, affection, intelligence, and responsiveness are found in pedigreed Siamese cats.

Unpedigreed Siamese cats. There is a kind of Siamese cat without pedigree to trace its origin. It is characterized by a short tail or a tail with grotesque kinks, a chunky body, a round head and round eyes, a loud and unpleasant voice, and excessive restlessness and wildness; it may cry incessantly. Green or yellow eyes and white toes or feet are sometimes seen in these cats of unknown origin.

Unpedigreed Siamese cats are sold by dealers all over the world; the greatest number come from Siam and Paris.

Pedigreed and unpedigreed Siamese cats have been bred together; in countless cases the strains are hopelessly mixed. The characteristics are also mixed, producing very surprising results.

Siamese cats at cat shows. The novice should know that Siamese cats seen at shows are not always good Siamese or good specimens. Anything with Siamese markings is accepted; a white-toed or short-tailed cat will receive a ribbon if there is little or no competition.

Blue Point Siamese. Blue Points appear when certain strains of royal cats are bred together; this coloring is rare, because the blue character is recessive to the seal. There are light and dark specimens of Blue Points, as in the case of Seal Points. Don't attempt to lighten your Seal Point strain by breeding to a Blue Point; this will be accomplished only if you breed to a light specimen of Blue Point.

You can get all Blue Point kittens by breeding a Blue Point to a Blue Point. Breeding a Blue Point to a Seal Point which carries the blue heritage, or breeding together two Seal Points which carry the blue heritage, will give some Blue Point and some Seal Point kittens. (This may not be apparent in one litter.) A Seal Point that carries no blue will not throw a Blue Point kitten, even when bred to a Blue Point; some of the kittens from such a breeding will carry blue, and will throw Blue Point kittens when bred to a Blue Point or to another Seal Point carrying blue.

There is a Blue Point strain in cats coming very recently from the palace in Siam.

IX. RAISING KITTENS

WHEN a female cat comes into season it is spoken of as "calling." The cat rolls a great deal and cries in a peculiar voice used at no other time. A female cat does not call at regular intervals or for a definite period of time.

Breeders of Long-Hairs usually recommend not breeding the females under one year of age.

Siamese cats usually call very early, and it is seldom possible to hold them off until they are a year old. Try to take them through their first two calling periods, always; take them through the third, if possible. It is not advisable to let them injure their health by calling.

One or two litters a year is considered normal. Siamese call so hard and so often that it is sometimes necessary to let them have three litters a year.

If you have young male kittens in the house you should know that they have been known to breed as young as six months of age.

If your female is to be bred by your own male, when the time comes don't just turn them in together; allow him to breed her two or three times a day. Excessive breeding is very hard on both cats. One service is all that is necessary, as you will very soon learn if your cat is ever accidentally bred when you don't want her bred.

If your female must go away for breeding, she should be taken about the third day of calling; if taken sooner or later than that, the fright and excitement may cause her to stop calling.

In selecting a suitable mate for your female, pedigree is not the only consideration. The stud must be gentle, healthy, and free from parasites and skin trouble; the owner must be a reliable person who accepts only healthy females for breeding to her male; she must know how to care properly for a visiting cat. Avoid sending your female cat to anyone who accepts her without making sure she is healthy, and avoid those charging a low stud fee. A high standard is not maintained by such people. Almost anything can happen to your cat in the hands of people who are inexperienced or unreliable.

Don't ask the owner of a male to give you a breeding in exchange for a kitten. You cannot guarantee to raise the litter, nor can you guarantee that the kittens will be healthy and saleable. You should gladly pay a reasonable stud fee to the person who puts up with all the annoyances of keeping an unaltered male, and who makes it possible for you to get a breeding for your cat without running any risk of disease.

Be sure your cat's front claws are clipped before you send her for breeding. No matter how sweet and gentle she may be at home, she will be very difficult and cross with the male, particularly at her first breeding.

It sometimes happens that a breeding is not successful. It isn't anybody's fault. In this case, the owner of the female is entitled to another breeding; the cat should be sent the first time she calls. A cat with ovarian cysts may be sterile.

1

EQUIPMENT NECESSARY FOR RAISING KITTENS

A cage is the most convenient and essential item of equipment in kitten raising. Small cages are a convenience, but large ones at least six feet long are desirable. Such a cage is a whole apartment for mother cat and kittens; it contains bed, pan, and low flat-topped log on which kittens can learn naturally to sharpen their claws on wood. During the last weeks of her pregnancy the mother can spend much time in the cage, eliminating the danger of jumping from high places and the danger of squabbles with other cats. She gets the idea that it is her home, and she is happy to have her kittens in the warm, sheltered bed in the dark end of the cage. In the actual raising of kittens, a large cage saves work, gives protection from draughts and accidents, and makes training easy.

In cold or irregularly heated apartments an electric heating pad is often most handy; placed back of or under the bed, it is safe from claws or water; turned low, it gives an even and gentle heat.

Small, heavy, flat-bottomed bowls are part of your kitten equipment; these will not tip over easily, and the kittens can reach into them to drink; being heavy, they will retain heat longer, keeping the food warm. In the cage it is advisable to place the water bowl in the corner of the pan; if it is tipped over, it will spill into the pan and not on the floor of the cage.

If you have no cage, the mother cat should have a sheltered box or bed, in a dark place free from draughts. If the bed has seven- or eight-inch sides, the kittens will not be able to climb over until they are old enough to be allowed out. Darkness is necessary when the kittens' eyes open; they must be accustomed to light gradually in order to avoid eye trouble.

It is essential that you and your cat agree on the place she is to have for her kittens; if you try to make her have her kittens in a place she does not like, she will never be satisfied and will be forever dragging them about.

The cat starts looking for a bed a week or so before the kittens are due. It is easy to arrange some bed so attractive to her that she will think it was her own idea and her discovery.

2

CARE OF FEMALE CAT DURING PREGNANCY

The gestation period is approximately sixty-three days. The cat is usually placid and in excellent health during this time; she should be friendly with all other cats, but will become timid as she gets heavier, and other cats may mistreat her. She must be protected from this. As soon as her kittens are born she changes, becoming increasingly aggressive; by the time she is weaning them, she is so worn out and nervous that she may be cross with her own kittens.

A cat that is carrying kittens should not be picked up unless necessary, and then great care should be taken. She really should not be lifted at all, and certainly not by her neck or shoulders.

A female cat must be so well cared for and so well-nourished that she is strong and fine and in good condition each time she is bred. This means she must never be allowed to get pathetically thin; plenty of good nourishing food is not enough; she needs extra vitamin and calcium support. During gestation and lactation periods a female needs extra meals; she should have plenty of beef, milk, and eggs. Three weeks before the kittens are due calcium and Vitamins A and D should be added to her food and continued through the lactation period. Dr. Camuti's liquid vitamin tonic will produce a healthy litter and maintain a reserve of strength in the mother for future litters. (See section on Rickets.)

3

BIRTH OF KITTENS

Cats very seldom have any difficulty when their kittens are born. Well-loved house pets do not wish to go away and hide at this time; they want to be near the people they love.

A few days before the kittens are born the cat begins looking in a serious way for a suitable nest—which means she will turn completely upside down some bureau drawer or the nice nest you have prepared for her. It is advisable to use soft old cloths or towels in the nest, as they will be stained and require changing. Pretty blankets can be put in later.

Kittens are usually born at night, and the mother frequently refuses her dinner that evening. Older kittens must be kept away from this time on, as they will nurse the mother if they get a chance.

As a rule, kittens are born quite easily, within fifteen to thirty minutes of each other. If a cat is in labor four or five hours, the veterinarian should see her promptly. If a cat has had rickets, it is wise to have the veterinarian from the very first, for she probably has a narrow pelvis, making normal delivery impossible.

It is quite easy to determine whether everything is going along normally; if it is not, your veterinarian should be called.

The female cuts the cord herself, and usually eats the placenta. If a cat is very nervous she may make a mistake and injure the kittens; that is why she should have her kittens in her own home, where she is most apt to be quiet and happy.

If you keep your cat under observation during the birth of her first litter, you will have a very good idea what to expect from her in the future. Many cats manage nicely with no help, and are perfectly reliable.

Some cats lie on their kittens and smother them; this tendency, if present, will be discovered in the first litter, and the cat will always have to be watched. It is necessary to keep such a cat under constant observation for twenty-four hours. By that time the kittens are strong enough to cry when she lies on them, and if you are not too far away you will hear them and can go to their rescue. By the time they are a week old they should be able to crawl out by themselves.

If your cat has had a difficult time during the birth of her kittens and you fear there may still be a kitten unborn, by all means, have your veterinarian look at her.

There is a discharge for several days. If it is bright red, and odorless, that is normal; if it is dark red and has an offensive odor, the doctor must be called quickly.

As a rule, a cat eats very little for a few days after the birth of her kittens. If she has had a hard time, give her invalid food. If she has had no trouble, feed as usual.

Some kittens may be born dead; some may be too weak to survive long; keeping a kitten very warm will sometimes revive it.

Cats having their first litter before they are a year old often lose the whole litter.

If a cat is left with no kittens her milk must be dried up. This can be done by feeding two small meals a day, to which has been added as much epsom salt as the cat will tolerate; give very little fluids. Apply camphorated oil to the breasts three times daily for a few days, then twice daily; it is not necessary to rub very much, as the oil penetrates easily. If there is caking in spite of this treatment, the veterinarian must help you.

Sometimes young kittens fail to take enough milk and there is caking; watch for this.

Three kittens are as many as a cat can raise without drawing on the reserve which she should maintain for future litters. If you wish to raise a larger litter you should start feeding by hand at three weeks of age.

If a nursing mother shows weakness, inability to leap up and down, or perhaps paralysis of the rear quarters, have the doctor at once. The strain of the kittens is too great for her, and you will probably be advised not to try breeding her again.

If a kitten is born with a hernia it can be corrected.

4

CARE OF THE KITTENS

If all the other cats in the household are gentle and friendly you need have little fear of their hurting the kittens; usually, other cats are frightened to death of the kittens until they are a few weeks old.

For the first month there is nothing to do for the kittens but keep the temperature even, gradually increase the light, and keep the mother placid and happy. Kittens' eyes start opening the first week in most cases; sometimes there is matter in the eyes, causing them to stick almost before they open, so that unless you are observant you will think they have not yet opened. They can be gently cared for with a warm borax solution.

If you handle the kittens your hands should be warm, and the kittens should always be picked up in such a manner that they are not fearful of being dropped.

If the kittens have diarrhea it means the mother's milk is not right or the food you are giving is not correct.

If a mother cat refuses to eat away from her kittens her food can be served in a very deep dish right in the nest. Pick up food particles around the dish after she has finished.

At about one month of age kittens climb over the sides of their bed and start moving about; if they are in a cage they will start using the pan of their own accord. For a time they will continue to use the blankets also, but by constantly changing them, and by putting back a few soiled papers in the pan each time it is changed, you will soon have them using the pan exclusively. Sometimes after using the pan quite properly for several weeks, they decide to use the bed again. It may be necessary to switch the locations of bed and pan, or it may be necessary to make them sleep on paper until they have forgotten about using the blankets.

You must always watch for the chewing habit; the instant you find a hole in a blanket, take them all out and make the kittens sleep on paper.

Besides a large cage, kittens should have a fairly bare room at their disposal, a room with no rugs, books, drapes, or any of the things which tempt kittens to become destructive. By five or six weeks of age the kittens must begin to have play periods on the floor, and these periods must increase in length as they grow older. They will play strenuously, and the weaker ones of the litter should be put back in the cage first, so that the strong ones may use up their excessive energy on each other.

Make sure that chairs are so arranged that the kittens cannot get to heights from which they should not fall. Normal kittens cannot hurt each other in normal play.

Be very careful when holding or carrying kittens of one and two months of age. They will leap unexpectedly right out of your hands, and the distance to the floor is too great for them to fall.

The play schedule should be fairly regular. If they are left too long in the cage they will start eating paper or blankets through boredom. If they are left too long on the floor they will fall asleep wherever they happen to be when they become too tired to play; they may sleep in a draught and catch cold.

If kittens decide to use a corner of the cage or room, instead of their pan, just put a pan there temporarily.

Kittens have a daily, well-formed bowel movement. If they do not start using their pan about the time you begin to feed them, a little white vaseline daily will soon get results. They will like the taste of vaseline.

It is quite safe to clip kittens' claws; if kept clipped, they handle themselves perfectly.

5

WEANING KITTENS

A cage is very useful during the weaning period; kittens can be kept away from the mother, yet she can feel close to them. Shutting a mother cat into a room away from her kittens always gets her terribly upset.

Under normal conditions where the mother is strong and healthy and shows no strain, and where the supply of milk is adequate and of good quality, the teaching of kittens to eat is simple and easy; they are started at approximately a month of age with the thing most apt to agree with them, and the change from liquids to solids is gradual enough to avoid upsets.

The following table of approximate percentages explains why cow's milk is suitable as the first food to be given kittens.

	Cat	*Cow*	*Dog*	*Human*
Water	82%	87%	75%	88%
Fat	3%	4%	12½%	3%
Protein	9%	4%	7%	2%
Sugar	5%	5%	3½%	7%

Lime water is always added to milk or to any formula fed to kittens. It neutralizes acidity and prevents diarrhea. The proportion is usually one teaspoonful to a cup of milk, although two or three teaspoonfuls is sometimes needed; it is advisable to start very young kittens with a high proportion of lime water. Just bringing milk to a boil also makes it less laxative.

If lime water does not correct the looseness of the bowels, you can conclude that the food you are giving is wrong. Sometimes the mother's milk disagrees with kittens, causing colic or diarrhea.

No matter at what age milk is first offered to kittens, they seldom lap voluntarily. Actually, they must be taught to drink.

Everything given to kittens must, of course, be warm. For the first attempt, a small flat saucer is suitable; take a small quantity of milk, rub a little across the kitten's mouth so he can taste it, and then try to hold the dish so he can smell and lap without getting his nose in the milk; snuffing milk up his nose can't be a very pleasant experience.

If the kittens are separated from their mother a few

hours before feeding they will be hungry enough to take an interest in the food you offer; it will also be more likely to agree with them. They should be kept from their mother for a reasonable length of time after feeding.

When the kittens are taking several feedings of milk a day, and you are sure it is agreeing with them perfectly, the next step may well be one feeding daily of concentrated beef broth, made as for invalids. A few days will reveal whether this agrees with them. Finely minced, cooked beef can next be added to the broth, the proportion of beef being gradually increased. Scraped raw beef is suitable to use next. Some people give raw beef before giving cooked; but, as cooked beef agrees with invalids better than raw beef, it would seem that it would be more easily digested by young kittens.

While kittens are learning to eat solid food, their milk feedings are continued, and they are less often with their mother. It is seldom possible to leave milk down all the time, as it gets too cold, and kittens lose interest in what they see before them all the time.

A kitten which is slow about eating is the one most likely to take to eating blankets. Backward kittens should be fed by hand at frequent intervals.

When the kittens are taking solid food nicely, calcium and vitamins are added to the food; backward kittens get a larger amount. (See section on Rickets.)

As soon as kittens are eating beef well, it will be only a short time before they can join their mother in eating beef mixed with the prepared cat food, for she, also, will be getting calcium and extra vitamin supply if the kittens are still nursing. When the kittens start eating with the mother, the beef should be put through the grinder twice and the cat food should be boiled longer.

When the mother is eating fish, or something else the kittens do not have, they may have a meal of the prepared cat food alone, if it is not convenient to fix them the regular beef meal. The cat food makes a good meal for kittens; they usually like it, particularly if it is prepared in broth or milk.

As a rule, the problem is not so much how often or how much to feed, but how to get the kittens to stop playing long enough to eat. Almost every kitten presents his own individual problem, which must be met and solved. It is impossible to give a schedule of amounts and numbers of feedings for kittens of different ages; kittens and circumstances differ too greatly. Kittens should be neither fat nor pathetically thin; they should not be starved at meal time nor so overfed that they are uninterested. They should be kept strictly on wholesome, sensible food.

Feeding all the kittens together stimulates very young kittens to an interest in food. As they grow older it is more scientific to feed them separately, if it can possibly be managed. Each kitten can be watched more carefully, and you can send each one to his new home with an accurate feeding schedule which you know is correct.

At five or six months of age kittens can safely begin to eat vegetables and fish.

A raw egg beaten in warm milk is excellent to give the mother cat and kittens the first thing each morning, after the kittens are six or seven weeks old; as they get older two or three eggs may be required, if the litter is large.

As soon as kittens are eating solid food well, they may be allowed with the mother only at night; from then on weaning is very rapid. Kittens can easily be completely weaned by two months of age. During the weaning period, watch the mother closely to make sure that her supply of milk is decreasing properly.

By all means, no cat should nurse her kittens longer than three months; her milk has little value after that time, and she needs to begin building her strength for her next litter.

Kittens will sometimes nurse each other or some other cat in the house; it is hard to prevent this; examine the other cat to make sure no injury is resulting.

6

RAISING KITTENS BY HAND

Sickness or the death of a mother cat sometimes makes it necessary to feed kittens by hand from the first day.

Once in a great while a cat has insufficient milk or milk of a quality not nourishing to the kittens. (This is most apt to be the case with cats improperly fed.) As many cats appear to have little milk the first week, about the only thing one can do is watch the kittens closely. Normal kittens are active almost immediately, and within an hour after birth are yelling and fighting each other over a place to nurse. Sometimes you may be able to help late arrivals get their first food; they will soon have strength enough to hold their own. In small litters this should not be necessary. If a kitten is not active, cannot nurse, and whimpers, it is doubtful that anything can be done for him; a kitten too weak to nurse is probably too weak to live. If the whole litter whimpers and seems to be getting less active instead of more active, probably the mother has no milk; in that case you must start hand feeding at once.

The mother's first milk is very valuable to the kittens. If they can be with the mother at least long enough to get this, the chances of raising them by hand are much better. It is better to feed them entirely by hand than to try to combine artificial feeding with the mother's milk during the first week. Fortunately, if a cat has any milk at all she usually has sufficient for the first three weeks; the demand upon her during this period is not great. If you have a fine proven breeder, you need give no thought to these things.

Whenever kittens are given to a foster mother, it should be one whose kittens were born at the same time so that the milk quality will be the same. Such a cat must be healthy, and willing to accept strange kittens—rather a lot of difficulties to overcome in a very short time. Most people prefer hand feeding.

At three weeks you can supplement the mother's milk with hand feeding without fear of upset, or you can feed the kittens entirely by hand with good chances of success. Ordinary cow's milk is not sufficiently nourishing when kittens must be fed so young. Any good baby formula can be used. The following suggestion is a formula which has been successfully used from one day of age.

FORMULA

2 level teaspoonsful "Dextrose and Malted Wheat Germ Extract" (Squibb)
  Make a paste with milk
1 cup milk, added to above
  Bring to a boil
2 teaspoonfuls lime water, added when cool

At three or four weeks of age small amounts of calcium and Vitamins D and A are also added. (See section on Rickets.)

Whenever formula is being given to the kittens, the mother may be permitted to have all she wants. It will be good for her. This is a wonderful food for backward kittens of all ages.

A tiny, curved medicine dropper makes feeding easy. You judge the amount and number of feedings by the response of the kittens. Very young kittens can start with about one-quarter of a teaspoonful to each feeding, and they can be fed every hour or two; this must be regulated by how hungry they are at each feeding. Kittens will require night feeding, up to four or five weeks of age.

When they reach the excessively playful stage it is sometimes necessary to feed them when they are sleepy, or to wake them up for feeding, as they can think of nothing but play when they are wide awake.

From one month of age, the feeding proceeds much the same as described in the previous section. Kittens which have never had the benefit of their mother's milk can very well be kept on the formula until they are two or three months old. Once the kittens get to the point where they will lap voluntarily, the work is not so great.

7

SELLING KITTENS

Kittens should not go to their new homes under three months of age. Maternal immunity lasts to two months; kittens that do not pass out the first few days usually live to two months. The period between two and three months of age is critical, for it is then that the kitten is most apt to disclose whether or not he is strong and able to stand on his own.

If the kitten is to go to his new home with an accurate feeding schedule, it means he must have been completely weaned and on this schedule for a month before making the change.

The training of a kitten has hardly begun at two months; he may be using his pan properly, but the habit is not firmly established at that age. Kittens sold too young are the ones which most often become lax in their habits and which most often acquire the habit of eating blankets. The new owners usually are not sufficiently experienced to handle these matters properly, and the kittens acquire bad habits which can never be broken.

Kittens are not always ready to go into new homes at three months; an experienced breeder is able to determine this.

8

RESPONSIBILITY AFTER KITTENS ARE SOLD

Only by keeping in touch with the new owner can you be sure that your kitten is being properly cared for. It is necessary to be particularly careful that the feeding is right, that strong laxatives are not given, that the kitten is kept quiet, and that he is, under no consideration, carried into the street or in a car. People must also be warned particularly about open windows and about draughts.

9

ENLIGHTENED SELF-INTEREST IN KITTEN RAISING

The fact that a female cat may have three or four large litters a year does not mean that she is able to raise that number, even with the best food and care. Those who consider the good of the mother cat first will probably, in the end, raise the greatest number of healthy, saleable kittens.

If a cat is to be spayed after she has raised one or two litters, the number she is permitted to raise is not so important, provided she shows no strain.

A female that is to be used for breeding purposes must have her resources guarded and not have all her strength used up in the first few years of kitten bearing. It is for this reason that it is advisable to start supplementary feeding of kittens when they are three weeks old, whenever you wish to raise more than three kittens to a litter.

Between litters a female must recuperate from the last and gain strength for the next litter. For this reason, kittens should be promptly and definitely weaned, and it is important that the female have plenty of excellent food and all the calcium and vitamin support she needs. She should also have a quiet and happy home.

People sometimes think that because they are "not raising kittens to sell" they need not learn how to care properly for their female cat and her kittens. Unfortunately, the requirements of a mother cat are the same, no matter who is breeding her or why it is being done.

Spoiled cats that eat only tinned salmon or liver will not stand up well under the strain of raising kittens.

Cats usually have an excellent appetite during the gestation period, which makes it a favorable time to make corrective changes in the diet.

Pensioning females. Even the strongest females sometimes begin to show strain after five or six years of kitten raising; their health may begin to fail, their kittens may not be so strong or do so well; in particular, they may become irritable and cross and not at all happy individuals. Spaying such cats gives them back their health, their sweet tempers, and even their youthful trim lines. They become happy again and as playful as kittens.

10

STUD CATS

A male is most annoying during the period when he is maturing; this may be any time after seven or eight months of age, up to two years. Males are particularly difficult just after they have had a breeding. During these periods they spray and howl and are very restless. At other times they may be quiet and gentle but, since you cannot know just when a male may decide to spray, he can seldom be allowed in a room with a bed or any ordinary furnishings; since his temper is uncertain, he must be watched when there are guests, and great care must be taken about his cat companions. It is usually safest to let him enjoy their companionship through the bars of a cage or a screen door, at least when you are not present to watch him. It is absolutely impossible for a male to live with his mate, as he will breed her too often, so that she will always be having kittens; he will also attempt to breed her when she is carrying kittens, thus causing a miscarriage. Don't leave kittens with a male after they are about two months of age.

Be very careful about handling one male after you have handled another; you may be attacked.

A bare, sunny room and a cage will make it possible to keep a male in a home or an apartment. A gentle, placid cat is sometimes quite easy to keep. A nervous, highly-strung cat is extremely difficult, and may not make a good stud anyway.

Not all male cats make good studs. If you wish to have your stud at service, great care must be taken with his first few breedings. Male cats have bred as early as six months; while this is not advisable, there is no record of its having injured them. Breeders differ in their opinions as to when a male should be put at service, some saying one year, some two years of age. A few breedings before that time certainly cannot hurt a cat, provided he is not permitted to breed excessively. Studs held off too long before their first breedings seem to be the ones that will not breed a strange cat, but will wish to fight her. Things progress better if a male has his first few breedings before he reaches the fighting age; in this way he will get accustomed to strange cats coming for breeding. There is no reason for letting a cat of any age breed excessively; if you want your male to be quiet, breed him as little as possible. As three or four services are sufficient for a female at her first breeding, and one service for all others, there is nothing gained by just turning cats in together.

If your stud has much service, feed him extra meals and more beef and eggs.

It is not wise to put two young novices together, unless they live in the same house and are friends. A young male should have his first breeding with an older and experienced female who is not cross or difficult. A young female should go to an older male, sufficiently experienced to overcome her resistance and avoid her claws.

Your stud at service. Stud fees are payable in advance. You furnish a stud service certificate when the female returns home; the owner is entitled to a second breeding if the first one is not successful.

Handle all visiting females as little as possible; they are not reliable at such a time. Feed them what they are accustomed to at home; as a matter of fact, they eat very little, and the owners should never be surprised if they return home very thin. You should have a cage for visiting females, where they can get acquainted with the male through the bars of the cage before they are put together. You can determine from the response of both cats whether she is in season.

You cannot be expected to keep a female until she is through calling; keeping her over one night is reasonable; females have been known to call for two weeks after breeding.

11

SCIENTIFIC BREEDING

An intelligent breeder takes pride in the improvement of her strain of cats and in having an accurate knowledge of the rules governing heredity. This means an understanding of the Mendelian law, best acquired from reliable books on the breeding of farm animals.

The beginner should start with one female. Much must be learned by experience; suddenly acquiring many cats is confusing, and losses through sickness may be very great.

After the owner of one female has raised several litters she will know whether she has a good cat, whether she should retain some of her kittens for breeding purposes, and generally in what direction she wishes to expand.

While there is a market for fine cats, well raised, it does not come and knock at your door. It is best to raise only a few kittens while you are advertising and building up your market, so that your increased market will take care of your increased production.

Accidental breedings. If your pure-bred cat gets out and is accidentally bred to a stray, this will not affect subsequent breedings.

Inbreeding. Inbreeding is the breeding of closely related cats; it brings out the dominant characteristics of the cats bred; for this reason, only strong and healthy cats should be bred in this way. Very beautiful and strong animals are obtained from inbreeding when wise selections are made.

Size of litters. Some cats have large litters; some have small. It seems to run in the strain. Some cats are very irregular regarding the number of kittens produced. There is no scientific reason to believe that the male cat used has anything to do with the size of the litter.

X. TRAVELING

A CAT that travels little prefers a small snug carrier. Long-haired cats require the most room and the most ventilation; Siamese require the least room and the least ventilation. Most animal carriers are too large and have too much ventilation for cats.

No carrier or traveling case is suitable for journeys of all lengths or for all seasons and temperatures.

For long journeys, when cats must be shipped or sent in baggage cars, large wooden traveling cases are necessary. The bottom of such a case is filled with quantities of torn paper. The ventilation should be adjusted according to the time of year. No cat should be shipped in very cold or very hot weather.

In trains you are permitted to have your cat with you on the day coach or in a drawing room, provided, of course, you have a suitable carrier.

Taking a cat on the street or in a motor, in your arms, is subjecting him to great nervous strain and fright, unless he is accustomed to going out frequently. He may go into a panic and badly scratch the person holding him. He may even get away.

Every cat should have his own carrier, and it should not be loaned; the other cat might not be perfectly healthy.

It is an insult to a cat to transport him in a cardboard box; it is also dangerous, as he may get away.

Your cat should see his carrier often enough to be on good terms with it; he should be taken out in it frequently so that he will be accustomed to going and not be absolutely terrified when it is necessary for him to travel. If a cat is frightened or fusses badly in his carrier, it is usually best to pay no attention to him.

If your cat goes to the country with you in the summer, a delightful out-door run can be made of chicken wire.

A great deal of sunshine discolors a cat's coat, much as if he were acquiring a coat of tan. If your black cat gets rusty or your Siamese terribly dark, he will probably be quite normal again when he gets his new winter coat.

XI. COLLARS AND HARNESSES FOR CATS

THE thousands of cats wearing collars or harnesses are proof that they can do so as well as dogs.

1

COLLARS

Because of the ability of cats to wriggle out of any collar that isn't absolutely choking them, harnesses have been found much more suitable for taking them out on leads. Collars are for ornament, or to supply a means of putting a bell or identification disc on a cat.

Since cats climb about so much, they should wear safety collars which will break if caught on something.

Teaching a cat to wear a collar. The first thing a cat or kitten does is try to get a collar over his head, with the result that he gets it into his mouth. If his first collar is made of elastic it can quickly be slipped over his head and another attempt made. No cat must be left alone with his collar on before the owner is absolutely sure that he will not fuss with it. Do not put a bell or tag on a collar until the cat is fully accustomed to wearing it without one. Kittens wear their first collars at about two months of age. The first collar is quite snug. Cats look better with collars not so tight as dogs wear them, and cats accustomed to collars wear them quite loose.

2

HARNESSES

Cats seldom lead as dogs do; a harness and lead are more to give the owner some hold on the cat when motoring, or when exploring the garden or sunning on the roof. The cat does most of the leading.

Teaching a cat to wear a harness. A cat harness is light in weight and of simple construction. If a cat is accustomed to a collar, he should require only a day or two to walk naturally in a harness. The harness, like a collar, must not be left on when the cat is alone, until such time as he can be trusted not to fuss with it.

If a cat is to go out on a lead, he should start at an early age and go frequently; otherwise he will be terrified. A cat that is crying or growling all the time he is being led or carried about, is frightened and unhappy; if his owner really loves him, he will leave the cat at home.

Only gentle, placid cats should go out on a lead; neuters are most likely not to suffer by it.

The cat is a nervous, home-loving animal. When he must go somewhere, he is much safer in a carrier. A carrier offers the most suitable means of transporting a cat.

CAT SUPPLIES

AND

CAT DESIGN NOVELTIES

INDEX

INDEX

BEDS

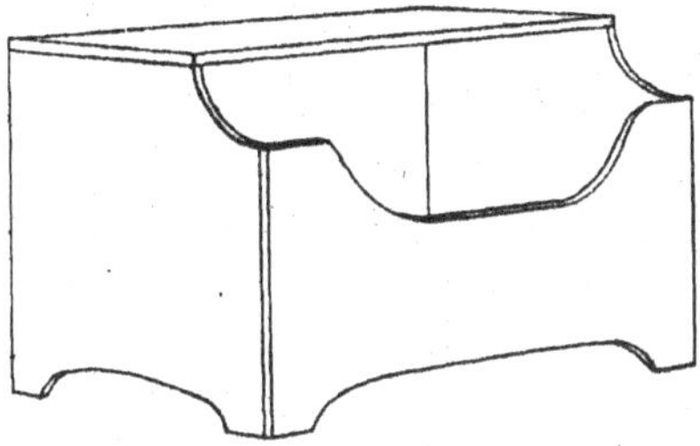

Small Bed - 12 in. x 16 in. $3.10
Medium Bed - 14 in. x 18 in. 3.60
Large Bed - 15 in. x 20 in. 4.10

Choice of light or dark finish.

f. o. b. N. Y. Shipped RailwayExpress. Free delivery in N. Y. C. and Brooklyn.

The small bed is suitable for any cat of ten pounds or less that likes a snug place to sleep. The large bed is big enough for a mother cat and kittens.

These covered wooden sleepers are practical beds of attractive modern design, providing protection from draughts. They appeal to cats for much the same reason that bureau drawers usually appeal to them. Cats frequently prefer them placed on a chair or table or a chest of drawers.

PADS. Cedarized kapok mattresses in green, green plaid, or red plaid.

Small size, 13 in. x 18 in. . 1.55
Medium size, 15 in. x 21 in. . 1.80
Large size, 16 in. x 23 in. . 2.00

Blankets for beds, page 2

✤ BLANKETS ✤

Finest quality, hand-made blankets, which launder perfectly. Approximate size, 23 in. x 36 in. Each, $1.00
Two blankets for $1.85

Choice of colors: red, green, medium blue, brown and tan.

Your cat will be more comfortable, and will look very beautiful, on one of these lovely blankets. They are suitable for use in carriers, traveling cases, cages and beds.

✤

BOOK

"Care, Feeding & Training of Cats"
Revised Edition 1.25

A practical handbook for cat owners, which tells how to prevent sickness through proper feeding and care. Complete sections on:

- Psychology and training.
- Feeding and care.
- Common ailments and common problems.
- Raising kittens.
- Breeds of cats and their special problems.
- Siamese Cats.

✤

BOOK MARKS

Cat Design

Assorted designs, six for 25

CAGES

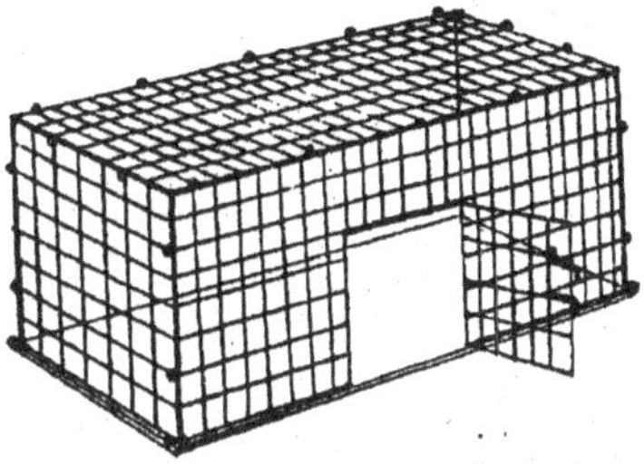

FOLDING WIRE CAGE

18 in. x 24 in. . . $6.95

18 in. x 32 in. . . . 7.95

Prices include Sanitary Trays.

Free delivery in New York City and Brooklyn.

A convenient light-weight cage, with wooden floor; easy to set up or take apart. A general utility cage which is particularly suitable for sun baths.

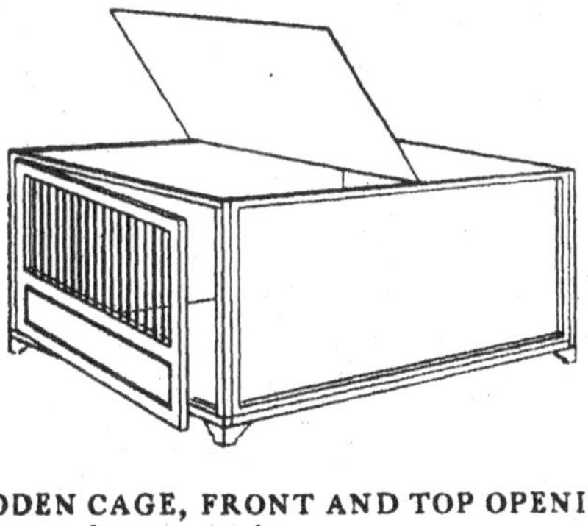

WOODEN CAGE, FRONT AND TOP OPENING

22 in. x 34 in. . . . 21.00

Price includes Sanitary Tray.

Free delivery in New York City only. Allow two weeks for delivery.

This excellent all-purpose cage is particularly suitable for raising kittens.

CARDS

Cat Design

Correspondence Cards - 15 for $ .25
Small Cards with envelopes - 15 for .25
Christmas Cards, assorted - 15 for 1.50
Greeting Cards, assorted - 15 for 1.50

This attractive assortment of Greeting Cards is for use during the entire year. It is made up of drawings and photographs, for all occasions, the year round.

CARRIERS

14-inch . . 1.95; 16-inch . . 2.20

Light-weight, black fibre carriers; ventilation at one end only. Suitable for kittens, Short-Hairs, Siamese. Excellent winter cases for all breeds.

Free delivery in New York City and Brooklyn, when part of a larger order. If ordered alone, the delivery charge is .25.

Elsewhere, the above prices are for Express shipment. If shipment is to be made by Parcel Post, allow for crating and postage as follows: 1st and 2nd zones, .68; 3rd zone, .77; 4th, .92; 5th, 1.09; 6th, 1.25; 7th, 1.45; 8th, 1.64.

CASES

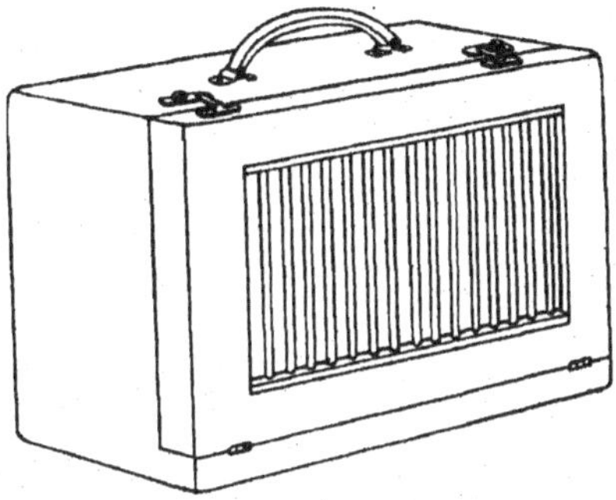

SMART TRAVELING CASES

20 in. x 10 in. x 12 in. . . . $6.45

Large enough for one or two cats; plenty of ventilation for long-haired cats.

24 in. x 14 in. x 14 in. 9.75

This extra-large case is for motoring and for shipping; there is room for a sanitary tray.

Free delivery in New York City and Brooklyn; elsewhere, sent Railway Express.

These attractive, strong cases are made of wood; dark finish; have locks and removable fronts for winter.

CATNIP

Fresh Catnip Leaves

Box 20
Large air-tight container . .50

Catnip is a tonic herb attractive to most cats. It is good for them to have a little each day.

CHRISTMAS SPECIALS

Christmas Cards . . . 15 for $1.50

General assortment of cat design cards.

12 Tags, 12 Seals, *Cat Design* . .35

Kitten's Christmas Stocking . 1.25

Selected small toys--bright, gay and colorful.

Cat's Christmas Stocking . . . 2.25

The newest cat toys; catnip leaves; special mice and fish and balls.

CLAW CLIPPERS

The correct clipper for cats, easy and safe to use. Made of the best hand forged steel. 2.25

A house cat does not need sharp claws. Because the claws of house cats grow abnormally long, it is advisable to cut them regularly.

COLLARS

COLLARS MADE ESPECIALLY FOR CATS

Be sure to state size.

Round Patent Braid - *red, green* 1.10

Crocheted Collars - *all colors* . . .50

Elastic Safety Collars . . .25

Safety Collar with two round bells 45

Safety Collar with one bell and name tag .45

Safety Collars are for cats that run out; they cannot hang themselves with these collars; they will break or slip off. These collars are not adjustable. Colors: black, brown, gray.

COLLARS

COLLARS MADE ESPECIALLY FOR CATS

Be sure to state size.

SPECIAL. Round Leather Collars . $ .30

Please give more than one color choice.

BELLS. Bells and Name Tags are attached to any collar, as desired.

Name Tag 10
Large Round Bell . . .10
Small Open Bell . . .10
Miniature Cow Bell . .30

If one bell or tag is ordered alone, please add .10, to cover cost of mailing.

COMBS & BRUSHES

The most effective brushes and combs for the elimination of loose hair.

COMBS

Steel combs, with set-in, rounded teeth.

A *real* cat comb takes out loose hair easily and quickly. These genuine cat combs are offered at the very low price of $1.00, each.

Very fine, short-tooth comb . . 1.00

This is a flea comb for all breeds of cats and a grooming comb for thick-coated Short-Hairs.

Medium spaced grooming comb 1.00

For Long-Hairs.

Coarse grooming comb . . 1.00

For very heavy coated Long-Hairs.

BRUSHES

Rubber brush - *red, green, yellow* .25

This brush is usually all that is required for grooming very sleek Short-Hairs and Siamese.

COMBS & BRUSHES

BRUSHES

Brush with short, stiff bristles $1.55
For short-haired cats.

Brush with long, white bristles 3.55
For long-haired cats.

Daily grooming is essential if a cat is to look beautiful and if he is to have the help he needs in the elimination of hair.

DISHES

Feeding Bowls - *red, green, yellow* .45
Water Bowls - *red, green, yellow* .60

DISINFECTANT

A general household deodorant and disinfectant, absolutely safe to use where there are cats.

In households where there are cats, this disinfectant should be added to all water used in wiping up the floors. A few drops in the sanitary tray each time it is washed, keep it free of odor.

6 oz., bottle . .75; 1 pt., tin . 1.50

In the 7th and 8th zones, please add .10, for each bottle and each tin, for postage.

FLEA POWDER

DR. CAMUTI'S FLEA POWDER FOR CATS

A highly effective, safe powder; you simply dust in the powder; no combing, brushing or bathing is necessary. . . . .60 & $1.00

F O O D

SUPPLEMENTARY CAT FOOD

1 lb. box . . .20; 5 lb. bag . . .75
Not postpaid. See postage rates below.

This is a balanced food which keeps cats regular; contains necessary minerals. An excellent food for kittens.

KIBBLED FOOD

In bulk, 1 lb. box .19; 5 lb. bag .75
Medium pieces only, 1 lb. box .30
Not postpaid. See postage rates below.

A very hard food that helps to keep cats' teeth strong. *This food is too hard for very young kittens, for very old cats, and for cats with poor teeth.*

Kibbled Food is also fed to the smaller breeds of dogs.

POSTAGE RATES

Zone	*1 lb.*	*2 lb.*	*3 lb.*	*5 lb.*	*6 lb.*	*10 lb.*
City	.08	.08	.09	.10	.10	.12
1st, 2nd	.10	.11	.12	.14	.15	.19
3rd	.11	.13	.15	.19	.21	.29
4th	.14	.17	.21	.28	.31	.45
5th	.17	.22	.27	.38	.43	.64
6th	.19	.26	.33	.47	.54	.82
7th	.23	.32	.41	.59	.68	1.04
8th	.26	.37	.48	.70	.81	1.25

Larger orders are sent Express.

GRAIN SEED

For those who wish their cats to have grass.

Grain seed grows readily in the house; it is cleaner than grass growing out-of-doors; it supplies tender blades which are not tough and harsh as grass often is. Box . . . $ .15

HARNESSES & LEADS

MADE ESPECIALLY FOR CATS

Simple, two-loop harnesses which do not hamper movements; one strap goes around the neck, the other around the body.

Give the measurement taken tightly around the body just back of the front legs.

Flat Leather - *moderately strong* 1.25
Red, green, blue, tan.

Patent Braid - *very strong, flexible* 3.45
Red, green.

SPECIAL. Sets for small cats 35
Small sizes for cats and kittens measuring 13 inches or less around the body. *State size.* Give more than one color choice.

JEWELRY

Cat Design

STERLING SILVER PINS

Hand-wrought, silver pins, attractive on blouse, coat, hat or purse. These pins make exceptional gifts.

Designs by M. Cone.

JEWELRY

STERLING SILVER PINS

A - $1.60

B - $1.85

Reproduced in actual size.

C - $2.55

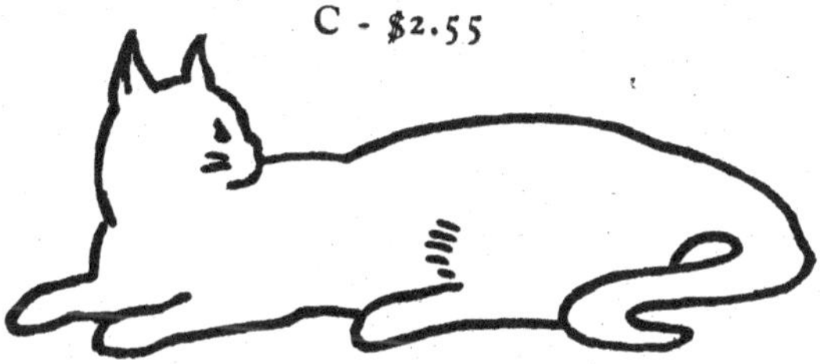

LAXAMEL

FOR THE ELIMINATION OF HAIR BALL

The modern, effective, safe lubricant for prevention and elimination of hair ball. By mail . . . . $ .75

If constipation is caused by an accumulation of hair, Laxamel will clear away the hair and help establish regularity.

Postage rates for Laxamel: City, .08; *1st, 2nd zones*, .10; *3rd*, .11; *4th*, .14; *5th*, .17; *6th*, .19; *7th*, .23; *8th*, .26.

PRESCRIPTIONS

DR. CAMUTI'S REMEDIES FOR CATS

Pre. No. 1 - Nausea Tablets
Pre. No. 2 - Corrective Laxative
Pre. No. 11 - Tape worm Remedy
Pre. No. 12 - Round worm Remedy
Above remedies, per vial . . $ .50
If one vial is ordered alone, the price is .55

Pre. No. 10 - Calcium Wafers .55
Supply necessary calcium to mother cats and kittens. Assure proper development and growth of kittens, proper bone growth, sound teeth; prevent rickets. Always given with *Pre. No. 14*

Pre. No. 14 - Vitamin Tonic . 1.00
2 bottles . 1.95; 3 bottles . 2.85
4 bottles . 3.70; 5 bottles . 4.50
Those living in 7th and 8th zones, please add .10 per bottle, for postage.
For building up cats that are below par, or to supply the vitamin requirements of any cat, this reconstructive tonic is unequaled. It is simply mixed with food; cats like it.

Pre. No. 16 - Disinfectant .75 & 1.50
Those living in 7th and 8th zones, please add .10 per bottle, for postage.

Pre. No. 20 - Flea Powder .60 & 1.00

Pre. No. 23 - Antiseptic Oil . 1.00
Should be applied instantly to scratches or wounds to prevent infection; clears minor skin irritations; is used in the treatment of ear mites.

SANITARY TRAYS

12 in. x 18 in., with 3-inch sides.

Aluminum finish $1.50
Enameled in apple green . . . 1.70
Any color, to order 2.20
Perforated Drain 95

Free delivery in New York City and Brooklyn. Elsewhere, the above prices are for Express shipment. If tray is to be sent parcel post, allow for crating and postage as follows: 1st and 2nd zones, .51; 3rd zone, .58; 4th, .70; 5th, .84; 6th, .96; 7th, 1.12; 8th, 1.27.

The above schedule is for a tray, or for a tray and a drain. If you wish to order a drain to fit in the tray you have, mailing charge is .30

Torn strips of newspaper are commonly used in trays for cats. Trays with inner drains are used both with and without newspaper.

SCRATCHING BOARDS

Carpet covered and catnip filled scratching boards, to be screwed to the wall or placed flat on the floor.

8 in. x 16 in. . 1.25; two for . 2.00
11 in. x 16 in. . 1.75; two for . 3.00

Cats enjoy these scratching boards so much that many cat owners think they should be listed as playthings.

SCRATCHING POSTS

"KATNIP TREE"

Large size - 28 in. high . . . $5.00

This is an exclusive, extra-heavy model. No cat can pull it over; very large cats can stretch to their full height when sharpening their claws.

This scratching post solves all problems of furniture scratching. It also makes cats very happy, and gives them healthful exercise.

It is natural and necessary for a cat to sharpen his claws. Providing a suitable post, which a cat *likes* to use, is as necessary as providing suitable food.

This large scratching post is the finest plaything a cat can own; and it is the most practical investment a cat owner can make.

Free delivery in New York City and Brooklyn. Elsewhere, the above price is for Express shipment. If scratching post is to be sent parcel post, allow for postage as follows: 1st and 2nd zones, .27; 3rd zone, .36; 4th, .52; 5th, .71; 6th, .87; 7th, 1.09; 8th, 1.29.

SPECIAL. Small Scratching Post . . 3.00

This is the post which regularly sells for $3.50. It is 20 inches high, and suitable for kittens and small cats.

Free delivery in New York City and Brooklyn. Elsewhere, the above price is for Express shipment. If post is to be sent parcel post, allow for postage as follows: 1st and 2nd zones, .16, 3rd, .23; 4th, .35; 5th, .49; 6th, .61; 7th, .77; 8th, .92.

TOYS

PLAYTHINGS FOR CATS

Provide fun and healthful exercise.

BALLS

Catnip Balls with rattle - 3 for $ .30
Catnip Balls on elastic - 2 for . .25
Cellophane Balls, all colors - 5 for .25
Crocheted Cellophane Balls - 2 for .30
Crocheted Ball, on cord, with bell .25
Celluloid-Rattle Balls, in all colors:
Three large *or* six small 30
Celluloid-Rattle Balls, on cords - 2 for . .35
Celluloid-Catnip Ball, red, green, yellow .25
Small Rubber Balls - five for 25

CATNIP MICE

Made with fresh catnip.

Box of two large *or* three small .30
Velvet Mice, medium size - 2 for .50

CATNIP FISH

New and very popular toys.

One large *or* two small Fish . . .50

PLAY STICKS

Stick with large *or* small rattle ball .25
With crocheted cellophane ball .30
With long streamers of cellophane .35
Add .10 for mailing one, two or three sticks.

SPECIAL TOYS

Mechanical Moth *or* Beetle 25
Mechanical Mouse 80
Catnip Snake, 26 inches long 95
Catnip Devil Doll, bright red . . .65
Box of Spider toys 30

ASSORTMENTS

KITTEN SELECTION. Play stick, small mouse, spider, small toys, balls to hang up .85
GROWN CAT SELECTION. Catnip surprise box, large fish, balls of all types, spider, catnip mouse, play stick 2.10
Kitten's CHRISTMAS STOCKING 1.25
Cat's CHRISTMAS STOCKING . 2.25

VITAMIN TONIC

Dr. Camuti's Vitamin Tonic is prepared especially for cats and supplies essential vitamins.

Keep your cat well by giving several bottles of this tonic each year.

For mother cats, growing kittens, and cats below par, this tonic is unequaled. It stimulates appetite and improves health. It is simply mixed with food; cats like it.

1 bottle $1.00
2 bottles . 1.95; 3 bottles . 2.85
4 bottles . 3.70; 5 bottles . 4.50

Those living in 7th and 8th zones, please add .10 per bottle, for postage.

WRITING PAPER

Cat Design

Box of 15 sheets 50

CPSIA information can be obtained
at www.ICGtesting.com
Printed in the USA
LVHW111411140819
627619LV00001B/65/P

9 781447 419570